NEW DIRECTIONS FOR CHILD DEVELOPMENT

William Damon, *Brown University*
EDITOR-IN-CHIEF

Infant Stress and Coping

Michael Lewis
*University of Medicine
and Dentistry of New Jersey*

John Worobey
Rutgers University

EDITORS

Number 45, Fall 1989

JOSSEY-BASS INC., PUBLISHERS
San Francisco • Oxford

Infant Stress and Coping.
Michael Lewis, John Worobey (eds.).
New Directions for Child Development, no. 45.

NEW DIRECTIONS FOR CHILD DEVELOPMENT
William Damon, Editor-in-Chief

Copyright © 1989 by Jossey-Bass Inc., Publishers
and
Jossey-Bass Limited

Copyright under International, Pan American, and Universal Copyright Conventions. All rights reserved. No part of this issue may be reproduced in any form—except for a brief quotation (not to exceed 500 words) in a review or professional work—without permission in writing from the publishers.

NEW DIRECTIONS FOR CHILD DEVELOPMENT is part of The Jossey-Bass Social and Behavioral Science Series and is published quarterly by Jossey-Bass Inc., Publishers (publication number USPS 494-090). Second-class postage paid at San Francisco, California, and at additional mailing offices. Postmaster: Send address changes to Jossey-Bass Inc., Publishers, 350 Sansome Street, San Francisco, California 94104.

EDITORIAL CORRESPONDENCE should be sent to the Editor-in-Chief, William Damon, Department of Education, Box 1938, Brown University, Providence, Rhode Island 02912.

Library of Congress Catalog Card Number LC 85-644581

International Standard Serial Number ISSN 0195-2269

International Standard Book Number ISBN 1-55542-844-4

Manufactured in the United States of America. Printed on acid-free paper.

Contents

EDITORS' NOTES 1
Michael Lewis, John Worobey

1. Studies of the Human Infant's Adrenocortical Response to Potentially Stressful Events 3
Megan R. Gunnar
A functional adrenocortical system is needed to withstand stress, yet we know little about its psychological regulation in early development.

2. Stressors During Pregnancy and the Postnatal Period 19
Tiffany Field
Interventions that capitalize on the young infant's coping mechanisms can be simple and inexpensive, but nevertheless effective.

3. Behavioral Features of Early Reactivity: Antecedents and Consequences 33
Michael Lewis, John Worobey, David Thomas
Behavioral responses to stress are consistent over time and related to illness in the first two years of life.

4. Infant Response to Frustrating and Mildly Stressful Events: A Positive Look at Anger in the First Year 47
Nathan A. Fox
Response to frustration may serve as an important window on individual differences in infant coping style and anger expression.

5. Immunological Consequences of Maternal Separation in Infant Primates 65
Christopher L. Coe, Gabriele Lubach, William B. Ershler
Recent studies have established that the early rearing environment can influence the development and expression of immune responses.

NAME INDEX 93

SUBJECT INDEX 97

Editors' Notes

In recent years, a growing number of studies have focused on the concept of stress and how children cope with stress. The concept of stress encompasses both the nature of stressful events as well as the nature of the organism's response. Some events are apparently stressful for everyone (for example, the death of a parent). Other events are stressful for some individuals but not for others (for example, starting day care). Thus one difficulty in the study of stress is the variety of events that give rise to individuals' reactions.

Individuals' responses to a given stressful event also vary. Some children show strong facial and vocal responses but exhibit little neuroendocrine activity. Other children show large increases in hormonal behavior but exhibit little overt stress signaling. The phenomenon of stress is thus as complex as it is controversial, and the definitions of stress and coping are as varied as the methods employed in their measurement. With advances in hormonal analysis, for example, information derived from neuroendocrine activity can now supplement behavioral measures and parental reports. Indeed, techniques now available allow investigators to examine the stress response in early infancy and to relate individual differences to a variety of antecedent causes and outcomes. The present volume considers the major issues surrounding the phenomenon of stress in the study of infants from the developmental, biobehavioral, and psychosocial points of view. The contributions reflect current perspectives on the measurement and meaning of the stress response.

First, Megan R. Gunnar summarizes what is currently known about the psychobiology of the adrenocortical system. Her chapter addresses the relationship between behavioral distress and cortisol release.

Tiffany Field focuses on stressful events. She describes unusual stressors in the pre- and perinatal periods and examines how to reduce the stress associated with these perturbations. A particularly important stressor for the infant is the stress of the mother during pregnancy. Hence, techniques of anxiety reduction for mothers are emphasized within the context of stress reduction for preterm infants.

Michael Lewis and his colleagues outline a theory of reactivity and describe their investigation of the links between birth status and newborn distress. In addition, they focus on the persistence of stress over the first two months of life and how this relates to health outcomes at two years.

Nathan A. Fox examines individual differences in the ability of infants to cope with frustrations such as physical restraint and pacifier withdrawal. The predictive value of individual differences in response to stress is demonstrated in terms of the relationship between early response to frustration and later social behavior.

Finally, Christopher L. Coe and his associates consider the vulnerability to stress of young squirrel and Rhesus monkeys, therein providing a comparative perspective on the response to stress. In particular, the relationship between stress, especially early trauma, and the developing immune system is clarified.

Together these chapters show how stress can be measured and what situations constitute stressors. Moreover, they point to the utility of measuring individual differences and relating them to various social and health outcomes in infant development.

Michael Lewis
John Worobey
Editors

Michael Lewis is professor and chief of the Institute for the Study of Child Development, Robert Wood Johnson Medical School, University of Medicine and Dentistry of New Jersey.

John Worobey is associate professor of human development in the Department of Nutritional Sciences, Cook College/NJAES, Rutgers University.

Research on the functioning of the hypothalamic-pituitary-adrenocortical system in normal infants is reviewed. Special attention is paid to the environmental stimuli and psychological processes regulating the stress responses of this system.

Studies of the Human Infant's Adrenocortical Response to Potentially Stressful Events

Megan R. Gunnar

Since the pioneering work of Hans Selye (1936, 1950), activity of the pituitary-adrenocortical system has been viewed by some as nearly synonymous with the phenomenon of stress. The growing literature on adrenocortical responses to stressors in human adults and in infrahuman species indicates that this neuroendocrine system plays a central role in stress resistance, although the mechanisms involved are not completely understood (Frankenhaueser, 1979; Gunnar, 1986; Hennessy and Levine, 1979; Rose, 1980). Cortisol is the primary hormone produced by the adrenocortical system in humans. Humans and other mammals deprived of a functional adrenocortical system can survive for fairly long periods of time in protected environments; however, without replacement hormones they cannot tolerate physical or emotional perturbations or stressors (Tepperman, 1980). Cortisol thus plays an essential role in the individual's ability to cope with even the normal stressors of daily life. Indeed, its physiological effects are ubiquitous, influencing almost every organ and tissue of the body. One of its primary effects is stimulation of hepatic gluconeogenesis, thereby increasing the energy available to the organism in response to challenge. Another effect is suppression of inflammation and alteration of activity of the immune system. Recently, Munck, Guyre, and Holbrook (1984) have argued that this second effect reflects the

---

The writing of this manuscript was supported by an NIH Research Career Development Award, HD00712, to the author.

homeostatic role of cortisol; specifically, cortisol contributes to the suppression of the normal defense effects of other stress-sensitive systems so that these systems do not, in a sense, overshoot. A third effect of cortisol involves feedback to the brain, where it facilitates the learning of new behavior patterns (de Kloet and de Wied, 1980). Thus this hormone plays three roles in stress resistance: (1) It increases the energy available for action, (2) it modulates the effects of activity in other stress-sensitive systems, and (3) it facilitates learning. Given the centrality of this neuroendocrine system in Selye's (1950) stress theory, the focus on this system in stress research with adults and other mammalian species, and the importance of the stress-related functions of this system, an understanding of its regulation is clearly essential to our understanding of how young children and infants cope with stress.

In the past it has been difficult to study this system in normal healthy infants because the measurement of cortisol required either blood sampling, which is feasible and ethical only under certain restricted situations, or urine sampling, which cannot be done easily and reliably with infants. Recently, however, radioimmune assays have been refined to allow cortisol measurement in small samples of free-flowing saliva (Riad-Fahmy, Read, and Hughes, 1979). This refinement has made possible the study of this system in normal infants and children. In this chapter, I outline our current knowledge about the psychobiology of the adrenocortical system in human infants. However, before outlining these data, I briefly consider what is known about the regulation of the pituitary-adrenocortical system in mature organisms.

The Adult Adrenocortical Stress Response

Under nonstressful conditions, cortisol is released into circulation according to a circadian pattern of basal activity that is regulated by centers in the hypothalamus (Tepperman, 1980). (See Figure 1 for a diagram of the pituitary-adrenocortical system.) In humans, most basal secretion of cortisol occurs between 3 A.M. and 9 A.M. Under certain "stressful" conditions, however, this basal regulation is overridden and elevations in the level of cortisol are observed. These conditions include pain and tissue damage and "psychological" experiences. It is the nature of the psychological experiences that is currently being debated. According to one school of thought (Tennes and Mason, 1982), psychological stimuli trigger cortisol elevation by producing negative emotional states. Elevated levels of cortisol thus serve as indices of negative emotions. This view has stimulated much of the research on cortisol secretion in adults and is currently stimulating similar research in the field of child development. According to a second school of thought, however, elevations in cortisol are not triggered by negative emotion but rather by novelty and

**Figure 1. Schematic Diagram of the
Hypothalamic-Pituitary-Adrenocortical System**

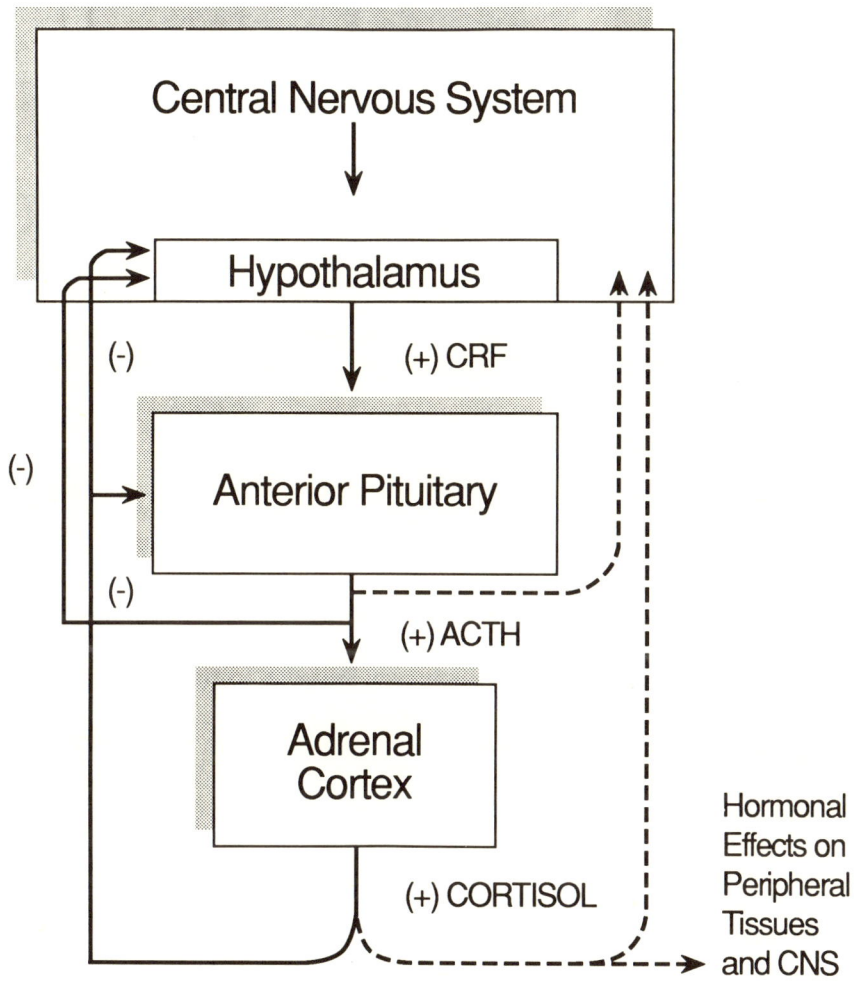

Note: The hypothalamic-pituitary-adrenocortical axis produces cortisol from the adrenal cortex. Solid lines represent feed-forward and feedback regulation; broken lines represent physiological effects. CRF = corticotropin releasing factor; ACTH = adrenocorticotropic hormone.

Source: Gunnar, 1986.

uncertainty (Levine, 1985). These researchers note that adrenocortical activity is often dissociated from negative emotional states. Furthermore, in human adults, cortisol elevations often quickly return to baseline following repeated or prolonged exposure to potentially stressful events, even though additional tests indicate that the adrenal gland is capable of continued responding (Rose, 1980). For example, Ursin, Baade, and Levine (1978) found that cortisol levels were highly elevated on the first day of parachute training in a group of Norwegian soldiers, but the levels were at baseline on the second day of training even though other stress-sensitive measures (for example, heart rate, adrenaline) continued to be elevated. Resolution of the argument over whether negative emotions or novelty and uncertainty serve as the psychological triggers of the adrenocortical response has not been achieved in the literature on adults. But data on infants tend to support some variants of the position that novelty and uncertainty are the relevant psychological stimuli.

Adrenocortical Activity in Newborns

Although the cortex of the adrenal is capable of producing cortisol fairly early in gestation, the structure and function of the fetal adrenal gland differs markedly from that of the adult. Approximately 80 percent of the fetal gland is composed of a fetal zone that serves to produce hormones necessary for the maintenance of pregnancy. This fetal zone rapidly involutes after birth, disappearing completely by six months of age (Hung, August, and Glasgow, 1978). Despite the presence of the fetal zone at birth and the corresponding immaturity of the zones responsible for cortisol production, the human newborn is capable of mounting a seemingly mature adrenocortical stress response. Indeed, we have been struck in our work by both the lability and the sensitivity of the neonatal adrenocortical system. As can be seen in Table 1, baseline cortisol concentrations following periods of sleep are quite low. Elevations in cortisol are produced by a variety of events, and there is some evidence that the response is graded. Perhaps the most striking aspect of the data in Table 1 is that elevations can be produced by such seemingly minor events as undressing, weighing and measuring, and discharge examinations. Does this mean that most handling of the newborn is stressful? If a statistically significant increase in cortisol from the low level of sleep concentrations is the definition of stress, then the answer may be yes. However, it is important to note that our concentrations in response to handling are similar to concentrations reported following periods of awake activity (Anders and others, 1970; Tennes and Carter, 1973). Thus, the change from plasma concentrations of 2 to 3 μg/dl to concentrations of 8 to 10 μg/dl may merely reflect a transition from concentrations supporting sleep to those needed to support awake behavior.

Table 1. Plasma Cortisol Concentrations Under Various Conditions in the Newborn

Condition	N	Cortisol
Resting undisturbed[b]	50	3.0 μg/dl
Resting undisturbed[c]	10	3.6 μg/dl
Resting undisturbed (before circumcision)[d]	80	5.2 μg/dl
Circumstraint board[c]	10	6.1 μg/dl
Vaginal delivery (cord blood)[a][e]	13	8.2 μg/dl
Discharge exam[b]	50	9.2 μg/dl
Weigh and measure[b]	20	10.4 μg/dl
High-risk delivery (cord blood)[a][f]	21	11.0 μg/dl
Heelstick blood sampling[b]	49	11.7 μg/dl
Circumcision by experienced physicians[g]	30	17.0 μg/dl
Circumcision by residents[h]	26	24.4 μg/dl
High-risk delivery (scalp vein blood)[f]	14	25.5 μg/dl

Note: With the exception of delivery, poststimulation samples were obtained at either twenty or thirty minutes following onset of stimulation. Resting undisturbed reflects over one hour of sleep. Before circumcision, many infants were more than three hours postprandial.

[a] Because of rapid conversion to cortisone, cord blood may underestimate cortisol response to labor and delivery.
[b] Data from two experiments: Gunnar, Connors, Isensee, and Wall (1988).
[c] Data from Malone, Gunnar, and Fisch (1985), Experiment 2.
[d] Data from Gunnar, Malone, Vance, and Fisch (1985).
[e] Data from Talbert, Pearlman, and Potter (1977).
[f] Data from Sybulski, Goldsmith, and Maughn (1975).
[g] Data from Gunnar, Malone, Vance, and Fisch (1985); and Stang and others (1988).
[h] Data from two experiments: Gunnar, Fisch, Korsvik, and Donhowe (1981); and Gunnar, Fisch, and Malone (1984). Residents had performed an average of five circumcisions.

In our work, we have explored several ways of differentiating "stress" responses of the newborn adrenocortical system from changes more accurately described as part of normal or nonstressed fluctuations. One promising approach is to consider the relation between unbound and bound cortisol in circulation. Under basal conditions, most of the cortisol in circulation is bound to protein and is biologically inactive. As cortisol concentrations increase, the ratio of unbound to bound stays roughly the same up to the point where the available binding sites for cortisol begin to be saturated. At that point there is a shift in ratio with increasingly more of the cortisol in circulation being unbound. In our work with newborns we have conducted a rough examination of these changing ratios by comparing concentrations of cortisol in plasma with concurrent measures of concentrations in saliva. Plasma concentrations reflect both bound and unbound fractions, while salivary concentrations reflect only the unbound fraction of cortisol. As can be seen in Figure 2, the shift in

Figure 2. Salivary Cortisol Concentrations in Newborns as a Function of Concurrent Plasma Cortisol Concentrations, in 5 μg/dl Intervals

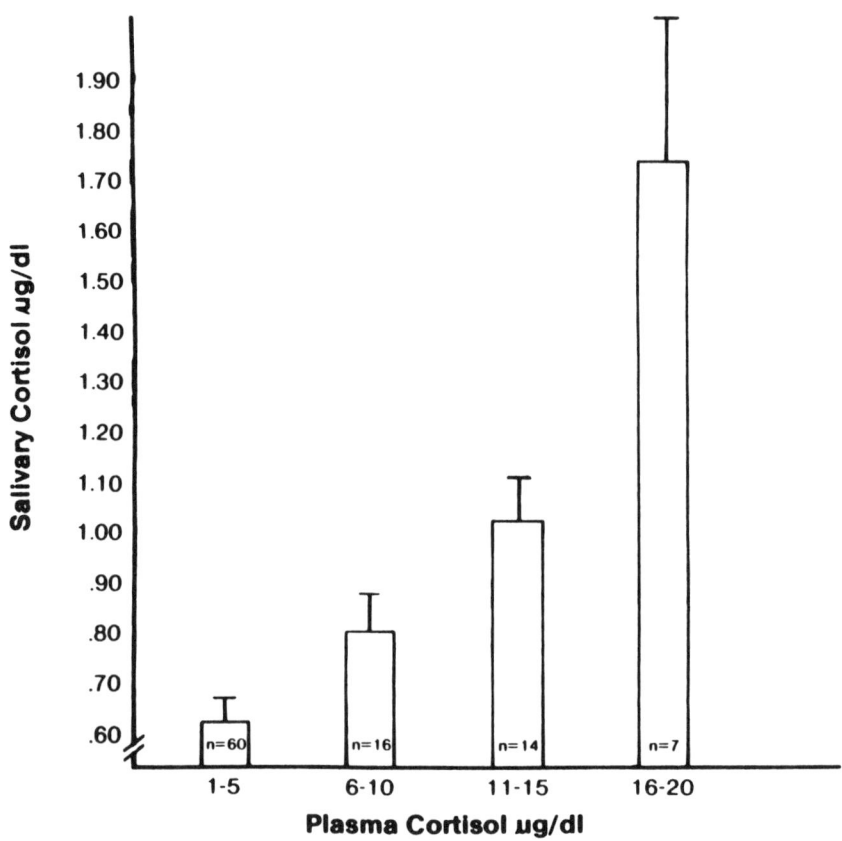

Source: Gunnar, Marvinney, Isensee, and Fisch, 1989.

ratio appears to occur when plasma concentrations reach approximately 16 μg/dl.

Having performed this analysis, we next considered the conceptual effects of reserving the "stress" label only for elevations to plasma concentrations of 16 μg/dl or greater. If we consider the normative data in Table 1, then of the events examined only circumcision and high-risk delivery can be described as clearly evoking a stress response of the adrenocortical system, on average. These events would certainly seem to be on a different scale of challenge than merely weighing and measuring the baby. In this regard the "16+" definition is conceptually meaningful. While circumcision provokes a fairly uniform response, all the other events we have studied have been associated with tremendous individual variations in reactions, with some newborns showing no changes from baseline even in response to blood sampling, and others showing poststimulation plasma concentrations of greater than 16 μg/dl after being weighed and measured. We have considered whether our behavioral data on these infants might be consistent with the 16+ definition of an adrenocortical stress response in the newborn.

The results of a reanalysis of our data were encouraging. We (Gunnar, Connors, Isensee, and Wall, 1988) previously reported that behavioral arousal and crying were positively correlated with plasma cortisol concentrations in healthy newborns in response to blood sampling, but that these measures were negatively correlated in response to either a discharge examination of weighing and measuring. We (Gunnar, Isensee, and Fust, 1987) had also reported positive correlations in extremely healthy newborns between cortisol concentrations in response to Neonatal Behavioral Assessment Scale (NBAS; Brazelton, 1973) and better scores on Lester's State Regulation Scale (Lester, Als, and Brazelton, 1982) whereas in slightly stressed newborns the positive correlation was between cortisol and behavioral distress. But when we grouped newborns in these studies according to posttest plasma cortisol concentrations (1-5, 6-10, 11-15, and 16+ μg/dl), in all instances we found that the differences in behavioral responding appeared, or were the most salient, only for the newborns in the 16+ μg/dl groups (see Figure 3). These data clearly indicate that adrenocortical activity does not reflect merely an increase in behavioral distress. Furthermore, they suggest that both withdrawing into quiescent states (Emde and others, 1971) and crying may serve as coping responses in the newborn, with each response being regulated in part by the stimulus. The data also support the idea that reserving the stress label for quite large increases in cortisol is conceptually useful in research on newborns. Whether this applies to work with older infants and children remains an open question. Furthermore, while these data are compelling, it is important to remember that they are the result of post hoc analyses. Replication is clearly needed.

Adrenocortical Studies with Older Infants

There have been only a few studies of adrenocortical activity and behavior in infants following the newborn period. I review some of them in this section, and several of the newer studies are discussed in a later section of this chapter. In this section I consider only the adrenocortical response to a classic psychological stressor, separation from the mother or primary attachment figure. It is well documented that children begin to be overtly distressed by separation during the second half of the first year of life. Behavioral distress reactions to separation typically persist throughout the second year and begin to wane in intensity and frequency during

10 INFANT STRESS AND COPING

Figure 3. Cortisol × Behavioral Response in Healthy Newborns

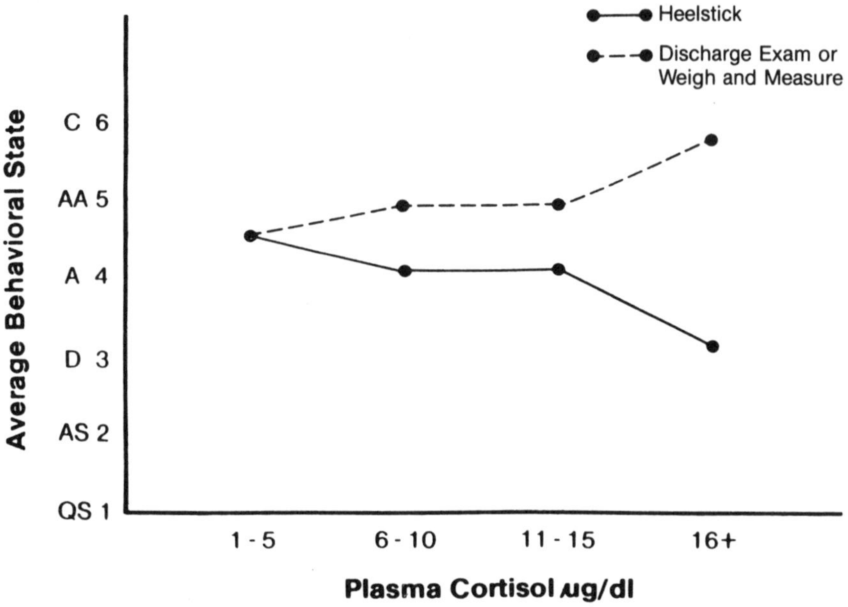

[Graph showing Average Behavioral State (y-axis: QS 1, AS 2, D 3, A 4, AA 5, C 6) vs. Plasma Cortisol μg/dl (x-axis: 1-5, 6-10, 11-15, 16+). Solid line: Heelstick. Dashed line: Discharge Exam or Weigh and Measure.]

Note: The behavioral states are as follows: QS = quiet sleep; AS = active sleep; D = drowsy/transitional; A = alert; AA = active alert; C = crying. Behavioral data reflect the weighted average of the percentage of time each state was coded.
Source: Gunnar, Marvinney, Isensee, and Fisch, 1989.

the third year. However, even in older children, a strange or threatening environment, illness, or fatigue can result in a resurgence of separation distress.

Most of the studies of the adrenocortical response to separation have been conducted with nonhuman primate infants. For rhesus monkey infants, separation produces tremendous three- to fourfold elevations in cortisol that decline back toward the baseline within twenty-four hours of the time of separation (Gunnar, Gonzales, Goodlin, and Levine, 1981). Similar increases have been reported in other monkey species (Coe, Mendoza, Smotherman, and Levine, 1978). To date, there have been only two studies of the separation adrenocortical response in human infants. A decade ago, Tennes, Downey, and Vernadakis (1977) took urinary measures of cortisol on twelve-month-olds on a nonseparation day in the home. They then repeated these measurements on a day when the mother left the house for an hour and the infant was cared for by a research assistant. Surprisingly, they found that although many of the babies were very upset by the separation, the event produced only a modest 20 percent increase in cortisol production, on average, and this was not statistically significant.

Recently, my students and I (Gunnar, Mangelsdorf, Larson, and Hertsgaard, 1989) examined the salivary cortisol response to separation in the laboratory. We used a long separation of forty minutes or more (Louisville Temperament Assessment; Matheny and Wilson, 1981) with nine-month-old infants; and with the same infants, a short separation of nine minutes (Strange Situation Assessment; Ainsworth and Wittig, 1969) at thirteen months of age. We found a statistically significant cortisol response only at nine months of age to the long separation (see Figure 4).

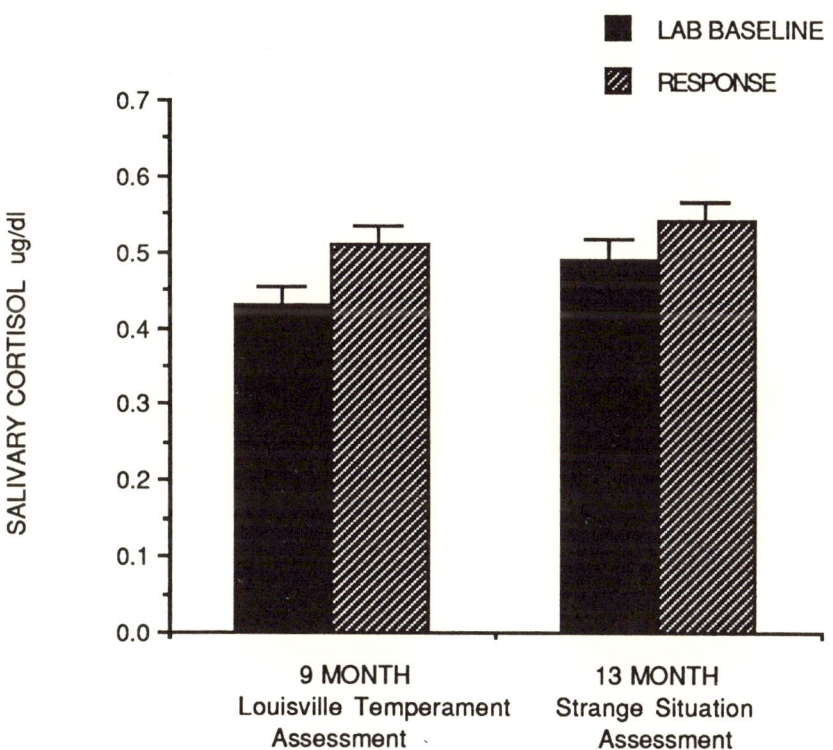

Figure 4. Salivary Cortisol Concentrations in Response to Maternal Separation in Human Infants

Note: Data are from the same infants, tested at nine and thirteen months of age. Louisville temperament assessment involves forty or more minutes of separation; strange situation assessment involves no more than nine minutes of separation.

Source: Gunnar, Mangelsdorf, Larson, and Hertsgaard, 1989. © American Psychological Association, 1989.

However, as in the Tennes, Downey, and Vernadakis (1977) study, even the increase at nine months was very small (20 percent), perhaps insufficient to be considered an actual stress response. This increment appears especially small when compared to the 300 to 400 percent increases seen in infant monkeys.

The meaning of these data is unclear. Compared to the newborn's labile adrenocortical system, perhaps the adrenocortical system of the older infant has become less labile or sensitive to stimulation. Alternatively, these data may indicate that the caregiving of research assistants who serve as babysitters buffers or prevents a full-blown adrenocortical response to separation in human infants. A third explanation is that separation may be a very familiar event for human infants by the end of the first year and that the adrenocortical response, as discussed earlier, may rapidly attenuate as the distressing situation becomes more familiar. There are now several studies with human infants that indicate familiarity or repetition of events can reduce the response of the infant pituitary-adrenocortical system as early as the first days of life.

Repetition and the Adrenocortical Response

We (Gunnar, Connors, and Isensee, 1989) recently completed a study of newborns in which we twice performed a discharge exam on the same babies on two consecutive days. On the first day, we obtained a statistically significant increase in cortisol, as we had in previous studies. On the second day, however, the discharge exam did not result in an increase in cortisol over concentrations obtained just prior to the exam. Because half of the babies were between twenty-four and forty-eight hours old on the first day of the study, and half were over forty-eight hours old, we were able to rule out the possibility that age or hours since delivery was responsible for attenuating the response. Instead, it appeared as if one prior experience with the discharge exam was sufficient to inhibit elevations in cortisol. This was very surprising and we are currently attempting to replicate these data. They are, however, remarkably similar to results recently reported by Lewis and Thomas (Lewis, 1988; Lewis and Thomas, in press). They examined salivary cortisol before and after inoculations in infants aged two, four, and six months. At two months of age, they found a significant and large elevation in salivary cortisol following inoculation. But, at four and six months of age, the average increase was small and not statistically significant. Although they studied different babies at each of these ages, the four-month-olds had also received inoculations at two months of age, and the six-month-olds had received them at two and four months of age. Thus, one interpretation of their data is that prior experience with inoculation inhibited or attenuated the adrenocortical response.

Finally, in a very recent study conducted by Gunnar, Hertsgaard, and Lehman (1989), we set out to explicitly examine the influence of experience on the adrenocortical response to novel experiences. The forty-eight babies in the study were between six and twelve months of age. They were tested twice a few days apart in a simulated swimming class for infants. Approximately a third of the babies were "experienced," meaning that they had been in or were currently in infant swimming classes. The remaining infants had never been swimming before. All were tested with their mothers, and the situation was designed to be very nonthreatening. We took measures of salivary cortisol at home and before and after each swimming class. Although we found no difference between the experienced and inexperienced groups, we did observe a change in response over our two days of testing. Specifically, posttest cortisol was higher on the first than on the second day. The difference was very slight, but it was statistically significant, again indicating that as little as one previous experience with a particular situation is sufficient to attenuate the adrenocortical response.

While these data are provocative, there are many more questions that need to be addressed before we fully understand the roles of novelty and experience in regulating activity of the adrenocortical system in infants. For ethical reasons, some of these questions may not be possible to address with human children as subjects. Perhaps the most important question has to do with the aversiveness of the experience. In all of the studies described above, even though the event might have been distressing, loving and caring adults were present to soothe the infants and respond to their signals. In a sense, while distressing, these were not situations that were overwhelming or completely uncontrollable. Unfortunately, for medical reasons or because of neglect and abuse, some infants do experience overwhelming, traumatic events. It is possible that recurrence of these events might not result in an attenuation of the response. In fact, in other mammals, recurrence of clearly traumatic events has been shown to sensitize or increase the adrenocortical response (Hennessy and Levine, 1979).

Individual Differences

Some of the most interesting questions about stress center on differences among individuals. Are there some babies who are more stress reactive than other babies? In the context of this chapter, this question is focused narrowly on the adrenocortical system. Thus, are there some babies who typically show a greater adrenocortical response than other babies to potentially stressful situations? As yet, we really do not have a good answer to this question. What is apparent, however, is that there is tremendous variability in the magnitude of the cortisol response within any sample of children tested. Thus, as noted earlier, during the newborn period some babies show no response even to blood sampling, and others respond dramatically even to being undressed, weighed, and measured. Similarly, even though the response to separation, on average, was quite small at nine and thirteen months of age, some infants showed dramatic increases while others showed no increases and even declines in cortisol following separation. What accounts for this variation?

Because there have been very few studies that have tested babies over time, and because the adrenocortical response may rapidly attenuate across recurrences of the same stimuli, we do not know whether the variation in response among infants reflects stable, enduring aspects of each child. We have found, however, that the magnitude of the adrenocortical response to separation is correlated modestly with measures of an infant's emotional temperament. Specifically, infants with negative emotional temperaments (withdrawal response to novelty, low adaptability, negative in mood) exhibit greater adrenocortical responses to separation than infants with positive emotional temperaments (Gunnar, Mangelsdorf, Larson, and Hertsgaard, 1989). On the surface at least, these data seem to support the theory that negative emotions serve as psychological triggers of the adrenocortical stress response. However, the evidence is equivocal because negative emotional temperaments at this age largely reflect negative responses to novel or uncertain events (for example, strangers and new places).

Another factor that may influence variation among infants in the magnitude of the cortisol response is the prestimulation level of cortisol. In our work with newborns, we make sure that the infants have been in a quiet state prior to our manipulations. We have thus obtained fairly homogenous and low prestimulation cortisol concentrations. For this reason, we have not found a correlation between prestimulation concentrations and the magnitude of the increases, or delta cortisol levels. Nonetheless, other researchers have found such a relationship in newborns and we have noted this relationship in our work with older infants. Specifically, Lewis and Thomas (in press) found that infants in their inoculation study who had high (but normal) preinoculation salivary cortisol levels showed less of an increase (and, in some cases, even a decrease) in cortisol following the inoculation than infants with low preinoculation salivary cortisol levels. Their data suggest that some of the individual variation is governed by the law of initial values (Wilder, 1956). Spangler, Meindel, and Grossman (1988) have noted an even more interesting relationship than that reported by Lewis and Thomas. Specifically, with newborns, they found that when multiple basal measures of salivary cortisol were obtained over two days, daily average cortisol concentrations were highly correlated. Furthermore, newborns with low and unvarying concentrations showed greater increases in cortisol response to the NBAS than did newborns with higher and more varying basal concentrations. In addition, these differences in basal activity were related to the newborns' behavior. Newborns with low and unvarying basal cortisol concentrations were more irritable in the nursery and more disorganized behaviorally during the NBAS exam. In a similar vein, we (Gunnar, Mangelsdorf, Larson, and Hertsgaard, 1989) found that although basal cortisol concentrations were not stable from nine to thirteen months of age, infants who at thirteen months of age had low basal concentrations showed greater elevations in cortisol in response to separation and also had more negative emotional temperaments than the thirteen-month-old infants who had high basal concentrations. These data may indicate that, within normal bounds, high normal basal or prestimulation cortisol concentrations reflect greater preparedness to handle challenge. As a result, perhaps the challenge is experienced as less distressing.

Summary

Research on the regulation of the adrenocortical response in normal, healthy human infants is still quite new. The refinement of radioimmune assays to allow the measurement of cortisol in small samples of saliva, however, promises to stimulate a marked increase in work in this area over the next few years. To summarize the work to date, we can be fairly certain of the following points: (1) The adrenocortical system is responsive to stimulation at birth, and elevations can be produced by a variety of normal events, including such seemingly minor stimuli as undressing, weighing, and measuring the newborn. (2) Increases in cortisol are not always associated with behavioral distress in the infant, and at times quiescence may be the behavior associated with large elevations in cortisol. (3) At least under certain conditions, the parameters of which are as yet undetermined, the adrenocortical system of the infant appears to rapidly habituate or attenuate its response with repeated exposures to the same event. As in any new area of work, the questions left unanswered are numerous. Minimally, we can ask the following: (1) Are there stable individual differences in adrenocortical reactivity? If there are, then when do they develop, what determines these differences, and are they related to the infant's behavior or temperament? (2) Are stressors such as separation from attachment figures capable of producing large increases in cortisol (that is, a clear stress response)? If they can, then under what conditions and at what ages? (3) Finally, what are the psychological triggers of the adrenocortical stress response in human infants? While the data seem to lean toward novelty and uncertainty, the possibility that negative emotional states play a role has not been clearly ruled out. These questions and others are likely to be the focus of much of the work in this area in the near future.

References

Ainsworth, M.D.S., and Wittig, B. A. "Attachment and the Exploratory Behavior of One-Year-Olds in a Strange Situation." In B. M. Foss (ed.), *Determinants of Infant Behavior.* Vol. 4. London: Methuen, 1969.

Anders, T., Sachar, E., Kream, J., Roffwarg, H., and Hellman, L. "Behavioral State and Plasma Cortisol Response in the Human Newborn." *Pediatrics,* 1970, 46, 532-537.

Brazelton, T. B. *Neonatal Behavioral Assessment Scale.* Clinics in Developmental Medicine, no. 88. Philadelphia: Lippincott, 1973.

Coe, C., Mendoza, S., Smotherman, W., and Levine, S. "Mother-Infant Attachment in the Squirrel Monkey: Adrenal Responses to Separation." *Behavioral Biology,* 1978, 22, 256-263.

De Kloet, R., and de Wied, D. "The Brain as Target Tissue for Hormones of Pituitary Origin: Behavioral and Biochemical Studies." In L. Martini and W. F. Ganong (eds.), *Frontiers in Neuroendocrinology.* Vol. 6. New York: Raven Press, 1980.

Emde, R. N., Harmon, R., Metcalf, D., Koenig, K., and Wagonfield, S. "Stress and Neonatal Sleep." *Psychosomatic Medicine,* 1971, 33, 491-497.

Frankenhaueser, M. "Psychoendocrine Approaches to the Study of Emotion as Related to Stress and Coping." In H. Howe and R. Dienstbier (eds.), *Nebraska Symposium on Motivation.* Lincoln: University of Nebraska Press, 1979.

Gunnar, M. "Human Developmental Psychoendocrinology: A Review of Research on Neuroendocrine Responses to Challenge and Threat in Infancy and Childhood." In M. Lamb, A. Brown, and B. Rogoff (eds.), *Advances in Developmental Psychology.* Vol. 4. Hillsdale, N.J.: Erlbaum, 1986.

Gunnar, M., Connors, J., and Isensee, J. "Lack of Stability in Neonatal Adrenocortical Reactivity Because of Rapid Habituation of the Adrenocortical Responses." *Developmental Psychology,* 1989, 22, 221-233.

Gunnar, M., Connors, J., Isensee, J., and Wall, L. "Adrenocortical Activity and Behavioral Distress in Human Newborns." *Developmental Psychobiology,* 1988, 21, 297-310.

Gunnar, M., Fisch, R., Korsvik, S., and Donhowe, J. "The Effect of Circumcision on Serum Cortisol and Behavior." *Psychoneuroendocrinology,* 1981, 6 (3), 269-276.

Gunnar, M., Fisch, R. O., and Malone, S. "The Effects of a Pacifying Stimulus on Behavioral and Adrenocortical Responses to Circumcision." *Journal of the American Academy of Child Psychiatry,* 1984, 23, 34-38.

Gunnar, M., Gonzales, C., Goodlin, B., and Levine, S. "Behavioral and Pituitary-Adrenal Responses During a Prolonged Separation Period in Infant Rhesus Macaques." *Psychoneuroendocrinology,* 1981, 6 (1), 65-75.

Gunnar, M. R., Hertsgaard, L., and Lehman, H. "Adrenocortical Reactions to New Experiences: Correlates with Emotional Responding and Temperament." Biennial meeting of the Society for Research in Child Development, Kansas City, Missouri, April 1989.

Gunnar, M., Isensee, J., and Fust, S. "Adrenocortical Activity and the Brazelton Neonatal Assessment Scale: Moderating Effects of the Newborn's Biomedical Status." *Child Development,* 1987, 58, 1448-1458.

Gunnar, M., Malone, S., Vance, G., and Fisch, R. O. "Coping with Aversive Stimulation in the Neonatal Period: Quiet Sleep and Levels of Plasma Cortisol During Recovery from Circumcision in Newborns." *Child Development,* 1985, 56, 824-834.

Gunnar, M., Mangelsdorf, S., Larson, M., and Hertsgaard, L. "Attachment, Temperament, and Adrenocortical Activity in Infancy: A Study of Psychoendocrine Regulation. *Developmental Psychology*, 1989, *25*, 355-363.

Gunnar, M., Marvinney, D., Isensee, J., and Fisch, R. O. "Coping with Uncertainty: New Models of the Relations Between Hormonal Behavioral and Cognitive Processes." In D. Palermo (ed.), *Coping with Uncertainty: Biological, Behavioral, and Developmental Perspectives*. Hillsdale, N.J.: Erlbaum, 1989.

Hennessy, J., and Levine, S. "Stress, Arousal, and the Pituitary-Adrenal System: A Psychoendocrine Model." In J. Sprague and A. Epstein (eds.), *Progress in Psychobiological and Physiological Psychology*. Vol. 8. New York: Academic Press, 1979.

Hung, W., August, G. P., and Glasgow, A. M. *Pediatric Endocrinology*. New York: Medical Examination, 1978.

Lester, B. M., Als, H., and Brazelton, T. B. "Regional Obstetric Anesthesia and Newborn Behavior: A Reanalysis Toward Synergistic Effects." *Child Development*, 1982, *53*, 687-692.

Levine, S. "A Definition of Stress?" In G. P. Moberg (ed.), *Animal Stress*. Bethesda, Md.: American Physiological Society, 1985.

Lewis, M. "Infants' Behavioral and Salivary Cortisol Response to Stress." *Infant Behavior and Development*, 1988, *11* (special ICIS issue), 457.

Lewis, M., and Thomas, D. "Cortisol Release in Infants in Response to Inoculation." *Child Development*, in press.

Malone, S., Gunnar, M., and Fisch, R. O. "Adrenocortical and Behavioral Responses to Physical Restraint and Blood Sampling in Human Neonates." *Developmental Psychobiology*, 1985, *18*, 435-446.

Matheny, A. P., and Wilson, R. S. "Developmental Tasks and Rating Scales for Laboratory Assessment of Infant Temperament." *JSAS Catalog of Selected Documents in Psychology*, 1981, *11*, 81-82.

Munck, A., Guyre, P. M., and Holbrook, N. J. "Physiological Functions of Glucocorticoids in Stress and Their Relations to Pharmacologic Actions." *Endocrine Review*, 1984, *5*, 25-44.

Riad-Fahmy, D., Read, G., and Hughes, I. A. "Corticosteroids." In C. H. Gray and U.H.T. James (eds.), *Hormones in the Blood*. Vol. 3. New York: Academic Press, 1979.

Rose, R. M. "Endocrine Responses to Stressful Psychological Events." *Advances in Psychoneuroendocrinology*. Psychiatric Clinics of North America, 1980, *3* (2), 251-276.

Selye, H. "A Syndrome Produced by Diverse Noxious Agents." *Nature*, 1936, *138*, 32-39.

Selye, H. *Stress: The Physiology and Pathology of Exposure to Stress*. Montreal: Acta Medical, 1950.

Spangler, G., Meindel, E., and Grossman, K. A. "Behavioral Organization and Adrenocortical Activity in Newborns and Infants." *Infant Behavior and Development*, 1988, *11* (special ICIS issue), 295.

Stang, H., Gunnar, M., Snellman, L., Condon, L., and Kestenbaum, R. "Local Anesthesia for Neonatal Circumcision: Effects on Distress and Cortisol Response." *Journal of the American Medical Association*, 1988, *259* (10), 1507-1511.

Sylbulski, S., Goldsmith, W., and Maughn, G. "Cortisol Levels of Fetal Scalp, Maternal, and Umbilical Cord Plasma." *Obstetrics and Gynecology*, 1975, *46*, 268-271.

Talbert, L., Pearlman, W., and Potter, H. D. "Maternal and Fetal Serum Levels of Total Cortisol and Cortisone, Unbound Cortisol, and Corticosteroid-Binding

Globulin in Vaginal Delivery and Cesarean Section." *American Journal of Obstetrics and Gynecology,* 1977, *129,* 781-786.

Tennes, K., and Carter, D. "Plasma Cortisol Levels and Behavioral States in Early Infancy." *Psychosomatic Medicine,* 1973, *35,* 121-128.

Tennes, K., Downey, K., and Vernadakis, A. "Urinary Cortisol Excretion Rates and Anxiety in Normal One-Year-Old Infants." *Psychosomatic Medicine,* 1977, *39,* 178-187.

Tennes, K., and Mason, J. "Developmental Psychoendocrinology: An Approach to the Study of Emotions." In C. Izard (ed.), *Measuring Emotions in Infants and Children.* Cambridge, England: Cambridge University Press, 1982.

Tepperman, J. *Metabolic and Endocrine Physiology.* (4th ed.) Chicago: Year Book Medical, 1980.

Ursin, H., Baade, E., and Levine, S. *Psychobiology of Stress.* New York: Academic Press, 1978.

Wilder, J. "The Law of Initial Value in Neurology and Psychiatry." *Journal of Nervous and Mental Disorders,* 1956, *125,* 73-86.

Megan R. Gunnar is associate professor at the Institute of Child Development, University of Minnesota.

For those medical procedures that are necessary with preterm infants, the question arises as to whether various forms of soothing stimulation can be applied during the procedures to alleviate their stressful effects.

Stressors During Pregnancy and the Postnatal Period

Tiffany Field

The life of the infant might be considered stressful from the moment of birth, and the infant's behavior from that moment onward might be viewed as a complex of coping responses. However, some infants experience unusual stress from pregnancy through the postnatal period and are especially called upon to exercise those coping responses. This chapter is about unusual stressors, how the infant naturally copes with them, and how caregivers can provide assistance. Included is a review of studies on ultrasound feedback to reduce pregnancy anxiety and fetal stress, non-nutritive sucking to alleviate the stress of invasive procedures such as heelsticks and gavage feeding, and massage to help infants in neonatal intensive care units (NICU) with their struggle for growth. All of these interventions are simple and inexpensive inasmuch as they either capitalize on the infant's own coping mechanisms or incorporate techniques that are natural extensions of existing medical procedures. Most importantly, they appear to be effective.

The author would like to thank the infants and mothers who participated in the studies and the researchers who assisted with data collection. This research was supported by NIMH Research Scientist Development Award #MH00331 and NIMH Basic Research Grant #MH40779. Reprint requests can be sent to Tiffany Field, University of Miami Medical School, Mailman Center for Child Development, P.O. Box 016820, Miami, Fla. 33101.

Ultrasound Feedback to Alleviate Fetal Stress

One of the earliest stressors affecting the fetus is pregnancy anxiety. Countless studies have documented unusually high fetal activity and subsequent neonatal irritability in infants whose mothers experienced high levels of pregnancy anxiety (see Grossman, Eichler, and Winickoff, 1980). Some of that anxiety is related to the woman's concern about whether the fetus is growing and developing normally. Because many pregnant women are given ultrasound examinations to monitor the growth and development of their fetuses, the ultrasound sessions can be used effectively to reassure anxious mothers about fetal normalcy. The ultrasonographer simply describes and visually illustrates on the ultrasound monitor those growth and development measures being assessed, thereby presumably alleviating that source of anxiety.

In a study by Field and others (1985), forty women who were scheduled to receive three ultrasound sessions during the last trimester of pregnancy were randomly assigned to one of two groups: those who actually received ultrasound feedback and those who were simply told that their fetuses were developing normally. For each mother in the ultrasound feedback group, the ultrasonographer pointed to the body parts and features of the fetus as she measured them on the ultrasound video monitor and verbally elaborated her observations on fetal growth and development throughout the session. Prior to these sessions the mothers were administered the Spielberger State/Trait Anxiety Scale (Spielberger, Gorsuch, and Lushene, 1970). Following the sessions each mother was given a time chart on which to record the number of hours of sleep that she had on the night prior to her visit to the clinic and the number of minutes her fetus moved during a half-hour sit-down period prior to going to sleep. In addition, the videotapes of the ultrasound sessions were coded for fetal trunk movements.

As can be seen in Table 1, positive effects were experienced by the primiparous women who received ultrasound feedback. While having similar levels of trait anxiety, this group showed lower levels of state anxiety than the mothers who did not receive feedback. They also reported less movement of the fetus and longer nighttime sleep. In addition, the feedback mothers experienced fewer obstetric complications, and their infants were born at a greater birth weight and at a higher ponderal index (suggesting less intrauterine growth deprivation). Their infants' Neonatal Behavioral Assessment Scale (NBAS) scores (Brazelton, 1973) were also superior (see Table 2). Thus, simply asking the ultrasonographer to talk out loud throughout the ultrasound sessions and highlight fetal features on the ultrasound monitor appeared to effectively reduce pregnancy anxiety, as well as fetal activity, which in turn probably contributed to each mother's ability to get more sleep. These changes in

Table 1. Means for Prenatal Measures

Measures	Feedback Primiparous	Feedback Multiparous	No Feedback Primiparous	No Feedback Multiparous	Effect and Significance
Ultrasound 1					
State anxiety	31 (7.6)	36 (9.1)	32 (10.6)	31 (7.4)	ns
Trait anxiety	36 (9.9)	46 (8.2)	38 (9.9)	40 (5.9)	I[a]
Ultrasound activity	17 (12.0)	21 (9.2)	18 (9.9)	21 (19.7)	ns
Food aversion	.69 (.5)	.75 (.5)	.75 (.5)	.57 (.5)	ns
Ultrasound 2					
State anxiety[b]	30 (6.5)	38 (10.4)	37 (7.2)	35 (8.3)	I[b]
Trait anxiety	36 (10.8)	48 (11.0)	37 (6.9)	39 (4.9)	I[a]
Ultrasound activity	3 (3.4)	4 (2.6)	3 (2.4)	4 (3.0)	ns
Movement	6 (5.9)	7 (4.5)	13 (7.6)	13 (6.3)	F[b]
Movement duration	5 (4.0)	10 (8.7)	5 (2.9)	4 (1.7)	I[a]
Sleep difficulties	.62 (.5)	.88 (.4)	.25 (.5)	.43 (.5)	F[b]
Hours sleep	8 (1.0)	8 (2.2)	8 (1.1)	7 (2.1)	ns
Dreams	1.2 (.4)	1.3 (.5)	1.3 (.5)	1.3 (.5)	ns
Ultrasound 3					
State anxiety	31 (5.8)	40 (9.8)	38 (5.5)	37 (4.9)	I[a]
Trait anxiety	38 (10.7)	47 (14.4)	39 (8.3)	39 (6.2)	I[a]
Ultrasound activity	10 (5.4)	8 (6.7)	10 (4.7)	7 (3.1)	ns
Movement	10 (6.9)	9 (4.1)	13 (7.2)	14 (5.8)	F[a]
Movement duration	4 (2.0)	7 (5.7)	8 (4.7)	8 (2.1)	I[a]
Sleep difficulties	.23 (.4)	.38 (.5)	.25 (.5)	.23 (.4)	ns
Hours sleep	9 (1.2)	9 (2.3)	8 (1.2)	7 (1.0)	F[a]
Dreams	1.8 (.4)	1.8 (.5)	1.2 (.4)	1.0 (.1)	F[b]
Food aversion	.38 (.5)	.38 (.5)	.75 (.5)	.86 (.38)	F[b]

Note: Standard deviations in parentheses; ns = not significant; N = 10 per group; I = feedback-by-parity interaction effect; F = feedback effect.

[a] $p < .05$.
[b] $p < .01$.

Source: Adapted from Field and others, 1985.

pregnancy state may have contributed to the better neonatal outcome in terms of both growth and developmental performance. It is not clear why these effects were limited to the primiparous women, but these women may be more receptive to feedback because they have less experience with pregnancy than multiparous women.

Stresses Associated with NICU Invasive Procedures

Another unusual stress in early development is premature birth, along with its attendant medical complications that require treatment in an NICU. Data on the stresses of the NICU environment are voluminous (Gottfried and Gaiter, 1985). As Jerold Lucey (p. xvii) noted in his foreword to the Gottfried and Gaiter volume, "The prematurely born infant

Table 2. Means for Perinatal Measures

| | Feedback | | No Feedback | | Effect and |
Measures	Primiparous	Multiparous	Primiparous	Multiparous	Significance
Obstetric complications[a]	127 (18)	106 (22)	110 (13)	117 (17)	I[b]
Postnatal complications[a]	154 (16)	143 (32)	146 (21)	151 (22)	ns
Birth weight	3462 (186)	3133 (348)	3229 (485)	3108 (202)	I[b]
Birth length	51 (1.5)	50 (.9)	51 (1.2)	50 (1.8)	P[b]
Ponderal index	2.61 (.2)	2.51 (.2)	2.43 (.3)	2.49 (.4)	I[b]
NBAS scores					
Habituation	5.9 (.9)	5.1 (.9)	4.6 (.7)	5.2 (.6)	I[c]
Orientation	5.4 (.7)	5.7 (.9)	5.4 (.7)	5.6 (.7)	ns
Motor	5.8 (.6)	4.8 (.7)	5.1 (.4)	5.2 (.6)	I[c]
Range of state	5.4 (.5)	3.5 (1.4)	4.3 (.5)	4.6 (.7)	I[c]
Regulation of state	5.0 (1.0)	5.2 (1.4)	4.7 (1.5)	5.1 (.7)	ns
Autonomic stability	6.7 (.3)	6.8 (.7)	6.5 (.3)	6.2 (.1)	ns
Abnormal reflexes	1.0 (.9)	2.6 (1.9)	1.3 (.7)	1.7 (1.0)	ns
Activity	7.1 (4.8)	7.9 (3.7)	7.4 (2.2)	7.7 (3.0)	ns

Note: Standard deviations in parentheses; ns = not significant; $N = 10$; I = feedback-by-parity interaction effect; F = feedback effect; P = parity effect.
[a] Higher number denotes fewer complications.
[b] $p < .05$.
[c] $p < .01$.
Source: Adapted from Field and others, 1985.

emerges into a hectic, cold, noisy and bright environment filled with mysterious equipment and peopled by masked strangers who try to help. Almost everything done to or for the infant is painful, and that pain can certainly be felt, although it cannot be communicated. The infant who must have an endotracheal tube cannot cry and is not fed by mouth for weeks. His or her feet are slashed periodically for blood samples. The infant's respirator roars away night and day keeping his or her lungs inflated and sustaining life—but at what price?"

Although the preterm neonate appears to be bombarded with multiple and continuous medical procedures, many of the behavioral and physiological effects of these stimuli have not yet been studied. In those few studies that have investigated the specific effects of invasive procedures on the preterm neonate, oxygen tension ($TcPO_2$) has been considered the critical measure. Decreases in $TcPO_2$ are cause for clinical concern, and such decreases are what invasive procedures appear to stimulate. As part of a large study on supplemental stimulation, we have monitored $TcPO_2$ during various invasive procedures (Morrow and Field, 1989). For example, during the insertion of the tube for gavage feedings (considered a necessary form of feeding by most neonatologists), $TcPO_2$ on average dropped 14 mm, a significant decrease. Similarly, during

Figure 1. Sample Tracing of Change in TcPO$_2$

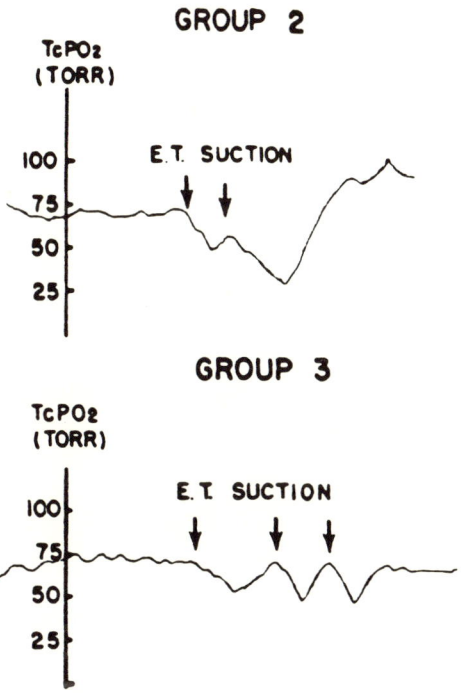

Note: This tracing of TcPO$_2$ is over time, following endotracheal (E.T.) suctioning for groups 2 (top) and 3 (bottom), respectively.

Source: Long, Alistair, Philip, and Lucey, 1980. Reproduced by permission of *Pediatrics*, 1980, *65*, p. 203.

heelstick procedures (again a necessary procedure for assaying bilirubin levels), oxygen tension again dropped on average 14 mm.

In a simple procedure to alleviate this problem, Long, Alistair, Philip, and Lucey (1980) instructed nursing personnel to use TcPO$_2$ monitoring to modify these procedures and to limit procedures that were considered "undesirable time," that is, procedural time that contributed to reduced TcPO$_2$. When monitoring was used, the amount of undesirable time was reduced from forty minutes to six minutes per twenty-hour intervals. Infants in the monitored group were handled less frequently and experienced less hypoxemia. An illustration of this can be seen in Figure 1, which shows that endotracheal suction in the group that was not monitored (group 2) caused a 50 torr decrease in TcPO$_2$, whereas insignificant decreases were noted in the group (group 3) that was carefully monitored during this invasive procedure. Thus, simply alerting the nursing staff to monitor the physiology of the neonate during invasive procedures appears to attenuate the stress associated with those procedures.

Our data (Morrow and Field, 1989), and those of Long, Alistair, Philip, and Lucey (1980), illustrate the physiological stress associated with such obviously stressful NICU procedures as heelsticks, gavage feeding, and endotracheal suction. Less obvious are the stressors associated with the removal of the infant from life-saving procedures, for example, weaning from the incubator. The stressful effects of weaning were another serendipitous finding in our supplemental stimulation study (Field, 1987). The protocol included plasma sampling via heelsticks on days one, five, nine, and ten of the stimulation study. The neonates were weaned from the ventilators one to two days prior to their participation in the study. As can be discerned from the data in Table 3, plasma levels of cortisol, a biochemical index of stress, were significantly higher on day one ($M = 61$ ng/ml) than on day five ($M = 41$ ng/ml). Because there was no significant difference among the levels of cortisol on days five, nine, and ten, which suggested stability of cortisol levels over that period, the data from these days were averaged and compared to day one. The percentage change from day one to the mean of days five, nine, and ten was a 25 percent ($p < .05$) decrease in cortisol values. Thus, although it would be important to investigate the difference between baseline levels taken prior to weaning from the ventilator and those taken subsequent to the procedure, these findings suggest that the weaning process is stressful. This is not surprising inasmuch as the infants have been dependent on life support systems and, with weaning, experience adjustment reactions. However, no apparent interventions are staged at the time of weaning to help neonates make those adjustments.

Table 3. Plasma Level of Cortisol (ng/ml) Following Weaning from Ventilator

Newborn	Day 1	Day 5	Percentage Change from Day 1
1	60	39 (41,37)	−35
2	47	25 (25,25)	−47
3	90	64 (68,61)	−29
4	33	32 (29,35)	− 3
5	34	30 (27,32)	−13
6	123	57 (67,47)	−54
7	38	42 (42,41)	+ 9
			−25

Note: Plasma samplings on days 9 and 10 are in parentheses, with the day-5 data. Standard error is ± 7; $p < .05$.

Source: Adapted from Field, 1987.

Even the simple developmental assessments that involve reflex testing and repositioning of the infant are stressful for the premature neonate. Although our TcPO$_2$ monitoring of premature neonates during the administration of the NBAS yielded no substantial decreases in TcPO$_2$ (see Table 4), other indicators of stress such as elevations of cortisol and decreases in growth hormone suggest that these assessments may be stressful (Morrow and Field, 1989). For example, data from a study by Gunnar, Isensee, and Fust (1987) suggest that cortisol levels were elevated following the administration of the NBAS to term neonates. Preterm neonates are also stressed when they are given the NBAS at approximately term gestational age. Again a serendipitous finding in our supplemental stimulation study (Field, 1987) suggests that preterm neonates are stressed during the NBAS, as manifested by a decrease in growth hormone levels.

Table 4. Average TcPO$_2$ Changes During Administration of NBAS

NBAS Items	TcPO$_2$	
Flashlight	+1.4	
Rattle	+1.6	$M = +1.7$ ($R = +1.4$ to $+2.0$)
Bell	+2.0	
Pinprick	-2.0	
Ankle clonus	-2.9	
Plantar grasp	-4.2	
Babinski	-6.6	
Undress	-6.3	
Passive arm movements	-5.6	
Passive leg movements	-4.7	$M = -4.3$ ($R = -2.0$ to -6.6)
Palmar grasp	-3.2	
Pull-to-sit	-4.8	
Standing	-6.0	
Walking	-4.4	
Placing	-4.7	
Incurvation	-2.1	
Crawling	-2.2	
Tonic neck deviation	+1.5	
Glabella	+1.0	$M = +1.4$ ($R = +.9$ to $+2.0$)
Rooting	+ .9	
Sucking	+2.0	
Inanimate visual	+5.3	
Inanimate auditory	+2.4	
Animate visual	+5.8	$M = +3.1$ ($R = 0$ to $+5.8$)
Animate auditory	+2.0	
Animate visual and auditory	0	
Cloth-on-face	+ .5	
Tonic neck reflex	+ .9	$M = +1.1$ ($R = +.5$ to $+1.8$)
Moro reflex	+1.8	

Note: Total mean change = -.7 ($R = -6.6$ to $+5.8$); $N = 22$.
Source: Morrow and Field, 1989.

Growth hormone levels have not been used to date as a physiological index of stress with preterm infants. While growth hormone values typically are elevated in stressed adults and children, stress-associated growth hormone levels are diminished in infants (Stubbe and Wolf, 1971). At the time of our neonatal assessment, the infants averaged thirty-six weeks in postconceptional age and sixteen hundred grams in weight. The infants were given heelsticks for plasma samples of growth hormone levels both on the day prior to the administration of the NBAS and two hours following the assessment. As can be discerned from the data in Table 5, the mean baseline value for plasma growth hormone was 21.5 ng/ml, and the mean post-NBAS value for the growth hormone was 14.4 ng/ml. The difference value ($M = -7.1$) was significant at $p < .02$. The 32 percent decrease in growth hormone following administration of the NBAS suggests that assessments of this kind are stressful for preterm newborns even when they are given just prior to discharge at approximately term age. Thus, these stressful experiences appear to be manifested by distress behavior and altered physiological and biochemical activity. These findings have contributed to the "minimal touch" policies adopted by many intensive care nurseries, which try to limit the number of stressful procedures as well as their periodicity. In addition, investigators are actively attempting to design less stressful assessments for the preterm neonate than currently used, with less handling as well as shorter assessment protocols (Als, Lester, Tronick, and Brazelton, 1982; Korner, 1986).

Neonatal Coping and Caregiving Activities that Help Alleviate Stress

For those medical procedures that are necessary, the question arises as to whether various forms of soothing stimulation can be applied during

Table 5. Plasma Level of Growth Hormone (ng/ml) at Baseline and Post-NBAS Assessment

Newborn	Baseline	Post-NBAS	Percentage Change
1	26.0	19.0	-27
2	20.0	12.0	-40
3	29.5	14.0	-53
4	19.5	9.0	-54
5	19.0	9.0	-24
6	25.0	19.0	- 4
7	13.5	13.0	- 4
8	19.5	19.0	- 5
			-32

Note: Standard error is ±7; $p < .02$.
Source: Adapted from Field, 1987.

the procedures to alleviate their stressful effects. Natural self-comforting behavior by the infant, such as nonnutritive sucking, and natural caregiving stimulation, such as stroking the infant, appear to be examples of effective alleviators of stressful NICU experiences.

The infant, on its own accord, apparently can effectively modulate stressful experiences by self-comforting behaviors. Because of the apparent effectiveness of nonnutritive sucking in calming neonates, we conducted a study in which NICU minimal care, preterm neonates were given pacifiers during heelsticks. The infants who were allowed to suck on the pacifier showed less fussiness and crying both during and after the procedures than those not given pacifiers (Field and Goldson, 1984). As can be seen in Table 6, the minimal care neonates who were provided pacifiers were less physiologically aroused by the heelstick procedure, as manifested by lower heart and respiration rates than the neonates who were not provided pacifiers. Although the NICU neonates who were given pacifiers also cried less, their heart and respiration rates were unaffected by the sucking treatment.

This inconsistency in the treatment effects on behavioral and physiological arousal was interpreted as a lack of cardiac-somatic coupling in the very immature NICU neonates. Thus, nonnutritive sucking during heelsticks appeared to attenuate behavioral distress in all neonates and physiological arousal in more mature neonates with less severe neonatal complications. This is not surprising inasmuch as sucking is conceivably incompatible with crying. However, this simple procedure is rarely used during stressful procedures such as heelsticks.

Gavage or tube feeding is another stressful procedure during which nonnutritive sucking appears to be an effective coping mechanism of the neonate. In another study from our lab (Field and others, 1982), a sample of fifty-seven infants admitted to the NICU were randomly assigned to nonnutritive sucking versus control groups. The groups were equivalent in gestational age (M = 32 wks), birth weight (M = 1300 g), and postnatal

Table 6. Measurement Means for Treatment and Control Groups in Minimal- and Intensive-Care Nurseries

Measures	Minimal Care			Intensive Care		
	Treatment	Control	p	Treatment	Control	p
Crying (% of time)	25	41	.005	1	19	.001
Heart rate (BPM)	172	187	.05	165	168	ns
Respiration rate	81	72	.05	51	54	ns

Note: All measurements were taken during heelsticks. Treatment group = infants given pacifiers for nonnutritive sucking; control group = infants without pacifiers; ns = not significant.

Source: Adapted from Field and Goldson, 1984.

complications. Neonates in the nonnutritive sucking group were given a pacifier during all tube feedings. Compared to the control group, the treatment group required fewer tube feedings, their average weight gain per day was greater, they were hospitalized fewer days, and their hospital costs were significantly lower (see Table 7). In addition, infants of the treatment group were easier to feed during later bottle feedings, as manifested by the nurses having to engage in fewer stimulating behaviors such as bottle jiggling and changes of feeding position.

In addition to infants coping with invasive procedures and stressful aspects of the NICU environment by their own self-comforting behaviors, caregivers can also provide effective comforting behaviors, such as stroking and body massage. One of the simplest interventions is touching by nursing or volunteer personnel. For example, in a study by Jay (1982), a clinical nurse specialist simply placed her hands on each infant's head and abdomen for twelve minutes, four times daily. The twelve-minute periods were planned around the infants' nursing and medical care to avoid interruption of the periods of touching. An objective of the intervention, according to the author, was to provide the NICU infant with periods of gentle human touch, during which the child would not experience coexisting painful stimuli. This simple placing of hands on the preterm neonate's head and abdomen was associated with a decreased need for mechanical ventilation, fewer startle responses, and fewer clenched fists of the stimulated infant.

In a more extensive touching intervention by our group (Field and others, 1986), we arranged for preterm neonates to have forty-five minutes per day, for ten days, of stroking and passive movements (a massagelike treatment). For this study, forty preterm neonates were assigned randomly to either a treatment or a control group. The groups were comparable in gestational age (M = 31 wks), birth weight (M = 1280 g), and duration of intensive care (M = 20 days). The neonates were selected at the time they

Table 7. Clinical Outcome Measurement Means
for Treatment and Control Groups

Measures	Treatment	Control	p
Number of tube feedings	219.0	246.0	.05
Days of tube feeding	26.0	29.0	.01
Daily weight gain (g)	19.3	16.5	.05
Number of hospital days	48.0	56.0	.05
Hospital cost (in dollars)	16,800.0	20,294.0	.01

Note: Treatment group = infants given pacifiers for nonnutritive sucking; control group = infants without pacifiers.

Source: Adapted from Field and others, 1984.

entered the transitional "grower" nursery. The treatment group received massage for three, fifteen-minute periods during three consecutive hours per day, for ten days. The stimulation sessions were comprised of three, five-minute phases. During the first and third phases, tactile stimulation or massagelike stroking was provided. The prone neonate received body stroking of the head and face region, neck and shoulder, back, legs, and arms for five, one-minute segments. The only region that was not massaged was the chest and abdomen owing to the neonates' apparent aversion to touching in these areas. We speculated that neonates may have formed an association between invasive procedures typically done in the chest and abdomen region and pain, and thus they preferred not to be massaged there. The next phase of the stimulation involved gentle flexing and extending of each supine infant's limbs. The final five-minute phase was a repeat of the first, massagelike stroking phase.

Clinical data, including formula intake and weight gain, were recorded daily. The neonates were given the NBAS and their sleep/wake behavior was coded at the end of the ten-day treatment period. The behavior observations were conducted over a forty-five-minute period, during which sleep states were coded as well as behaviors such as limb movements and facial expressions. The data analysis (see Table 8) suggested the following: (1) The stimulated infants averaged 47 percent greater weight gain per day, even though the groups did not differ in average formula intake (volume/calories); (2) the treatment infants were awake and active a greater percentage of the behavioral observation time; (3) the stimulated infants showed more mature habituation, orientation, motor

Table 8. Measurement Means for Preterm Neonate Treatment and Control Groups

Measures	Treatment	Control	p
Feedings (no. per day)	8.6	9.0	ns
Formula (ccs/kg per day)	171.0	166.0	ns
Calories (kg per day)	114.0	112.0	ns
Calories (per day)	169.0	165.0	ns
Weight gain (g per day)	25.0	17.0	.0005
Awake (% time)	16.0	7.0	.04
Movement (% time)	32.0	25.0	.04
NBAS scores			
Habituation	6.1	4.9	.02
Orientation	4.8	4.0	.02
Motor	4.7	4.2	.03
Range of state	4.6	3.9	.03

Note: Treatment group = infants receiving tactile/kinesthetic stimulation; control group = infants not receiving this stimulation; ns = not significant.

Source: Adapted from Field and others, 1986.

activity, and range of state behavior on the NBAS; and (4) the stimulated infants were hospitalized six days less than the control infants, which yielded an average hospital cost savings of $3,000 per infant. These data were recently replicated in a study by Scafidi and others (1989).

Thus, self-comforting stimulation such as nonnutritive sucking and natural caregiver stimulation such as gentle massage appear to attenuate distressed behavior and physiology during stressful NICU procedures. Inasmuch as these interventions are easily provided during invasive procedures, and inasmuch as they not only temporarily calm the distressed infant but also have positive side effects such as weight gain and abbreviated hospital stay, they would seem to be cost-effective ways of alleviating the stresses experienced by the NICU neonate.

References

Als, H., Lester, B. M., Tronick, E. Z., and Brazelton, T. B. "Toward a Research Instrument for the Assessment of Preterm Infants' Behavior (APIB)." In H. E. Fitzgerald, B. M. Lester, and M. W. Yogman (eds.), *Theory and Research in Behavioral Pediatrics.* Vol. 1. New York: Plenum, 1982.

Brazelton, T. B. *Neonatal Behavioral Assessment Scale.* Philadelphia: Lippincott, 1973.

Field, T. "Alleviating Stress in NICU Neonates." *Journal of the American Osteopathic Association,* 1987, *87,* 646-650.

Field, T., and Goldson, E. "Pacifying Effects of Nonnutritive Sucking on Term and Preterm Neonates During Heelstick Procedures." *Pediatrics,* 1984, *74,* 1012-1015.

Field, T., Ignatoff, E., Stringer, S., Brennan, J., Greenberg, R., Widmayer, S., and Anderson, G. "Nonnutritive Sucking During Tube Feedings: Effects on Preterm Neonates in an ICU." *Pediatrics,* 1982, *70,* 381-384.

Field, T., Sandberg, D., Quetel, T. A., Garcia, R., and Rosario, M. "Effects of Ultrasound Feedback on Pregnancy Anxiety, Fetal Activity, and Neonatal Outcome." *Obstetrics and Gynecology,* 1985, *66,* 525-528.

Field, T., Schanberg, S. M., Scafidi, F., Bauer, C. R., Vega-Lahr, N., Garcia, R., Nystrom, J., and Kuhn, C. M. "Tactile/Kinesthetic Stimulation Effects on Preterm Neonates." *Pediatrics,* 1986, *77,* 654-658.

Gottfried, A. W., and Gaiter, J. L. *Infant Stress Under Intensive Care.* Baltimore, Md.: University Park Press, 1985.

Grossman, F. K., Eichler, L. S., and Winickoff, S. A. *Pregnancy, Birth, and Parenthood: Adaptations of Mothers, Fathers, and Infants.* San Francisco: Jossey-Bass, 1980.

Gunnar, M. R., Isensee, J., and Fust, S. "Adrenocortical Activity and the Brazelton Neonatal Assessment Scale: Moderating Effects of the Newborn's Biobehavioral Status." *Child Development,* 1987, *58,* 1448-1458.

Jay, S. "The Effects of Gentle Human Touch on Mechanically Ventilated Very Short Gestation Infants." *Maternal-Child Nursing Journal,* 1982, *11,* 199-256.

Korner, A. *Neurobehavioral Maturity Assessment for Preterm Infants.* Unpublished manual, Stanford University, 1986.

Long, J. G., Alistair, G. S., Philip, A.G.S., and Lucey, J. F. "Excessive Handling as a Cause of Hypoxemia." *Pediatrics,* 1980, *65,* 203-207.

Morrow, C., and Field, T. "Invasive Procedures Reduce Oxygen Tension." Unpublished paper, 1989.

Scafidi, F., Field, T., Schanberg, S., Bauer, C., Tucci, K., Roberts, J., and Kuhn, C. M. "Massage Stimulates Greater Activity and Growth in Preterm Infants." Unpublished paper, 1989.

Spielberger, C. D., Gorsuch, R. L., and Lushene, R. E. *The State-Trait Anxiety Inventory.* Palo Alto, Calif.: Consulting Psychologists Press, 1970.

Stubbe, P., and Wolf, M. "The Effect of Stress on Growth Hormone, Glucose, and Glycerol Levels in Newborn Infants." *Hormone Metabolism Research,* 1971, *3,* 175–179.

Tiffany Field is professor of pediatrics, psychology, and psychiatry at the Mailman Center for Child Development, University of Miami Medical School.

An emergent literature suggests that procedures such as heelsticks and inoculations are acutely painful to infants and induce a stress response of sufficient magnitude to be useful in the study of individual differences in reactivity.

Behavioral Features of Early Reactivity: Antecedents and Consequences

Michael Lewis, John Worobey, David Thomas

Evidence from both anecdotal reports and studies that examine normal responses to everyday events indicates wide individual differences in infant reactivity and irritability. Numerous investigators have demonstrated that as early as the first few days after birth, normal newborns differ markedly in their fussiness and consolability (Birns, Barten, and Bridger, 1969; Worobey, Laub, and Schilmoeller, 1983). As a major part of the newborn's repertoire, crying is a biologically rooted mechanism for coping with distress (Lipsitt, 1983). Furthermore, assessment devices that attempt to globally evaluate newborn functioning across situations generally include an irritability cluster (Brazelton, 1984; Riese, 1983). In fact, regardless of the perspective represented within the growing literature on temperament (see, for example, Bates, 1987; Goldsmith and others, 1987), almost every framework that purports to describe behavioral differences across infants includes a dimension of intensity (Thomas and Chess, 1977), distress (Rothbart and Derryberry, 1981), or emotionality (Buss and Plomin, 1984).

The dimension of reactivity to stress warrants special consideration. For example, current treatises on the construct of temperament have identified reactivity as perhaps the central aspect of individual differences (Goldsmith and Campos, 1986; Rothbart and Derryberry, 1981).

Lewis (in press) has recently proposed that three features of the nervous system—*threshold, dampening,* and *reactivation*—not only are at the core of what defines temperament but also allow for the clear measurement of individual differences in reactivity. Within this view, threshold represents the level of stimulation necessary to elicit a response. For some infants the threshold may be very low, that is, almost any level of stimulation will produce a response, whereas in other infants a more intensive stimulus may be necessary before the threshold is reached. Dampening is the ability of the nervous system to stop or inhibit a response once it occurs. While threshold refers to the activation of a response, dampening refers to its cessation. Reactivation is the infant's ability to exhibit arousal again after dampening has occurred, and the feature is measured by a change in responding after repeated stimulation.

The identification of these features, then, at a time in the infant's life before much socialization has taken place, would seem to be a useful point of departure in describing the earliest individual differences in reaction to environmental events. A focus on reactivity has the added strength of allowing for objective measurement beyond an exclusive reliance on parental reports.

Although the features of reactivity outlined above may be displayed in response to positive or negative stimuli, increased attention has been paid to the reactions of the infant to aversive events (Anand and Hickey, 1987; D'Apolito, 1984). In particular, crying and fussing in response to a noxious stimulus allow for the examination of reactivity under quasi-naturalistic conditions. The medical procedures of standard well-baby care provide for such an opportunity, as infants are routinely subjected to aversive stimuli during their first year of postpartum life. Recognizing the illustrative potential of these necessary perturbations, investigators have examined infant responses to heelsticks (Field and Goldson, 1984), circumcision (Gunnar, Malone, Vance, and Fisch, 1985), and inoculations (Craig, McMahon, Morison, and Zaskow, 1984; Izard, Hembree, Dougherty, and Spizzirri, 1983; Izard, Hembree, and Huebner, 1987; Lewis and Thomas, in press).

The Use of the Heelstick Paradigm

In order to screen for hereditary and metabolic disorders, the newborns of nearly all modern nations are lanced in the heel to draw blood. The heelstick procedure takes only a few minutes and, relevant to research with males, is administered prior to circumcision. Moreover, the procedure is fairly well standardized; each infant is lanced in a routinized manner at approximately the same age (two or three days postpartum), usually just prior to the baby's departure from the hospital. Hence, the paradigm not only offers the possibility of obtaining data on responses to stress in very young infants but also does so in a culture-fair manner, before the influence of familial socialization.

As early as 1970, investigators used this procedure to examine individual differences in behavioral state and plasma cortisol in response to the lancing itself (Anders and others, 1970; Tennes and Carter, 1973). More recently, efforts have been extended to assessing the impact of the heelstick on the expression of pain (Grunau and Craig, 1987; Franck, 1986) and examining ways to reduce its sensation (Field and Goldson, 1984). Thus, an emergent literature suggests that procedures such as heelsticks are indeed acutely painful in newborns and induce a stress response of sufficient magnitude to be useful in the study of individual differences in reactivity.

In this chapter, we describe the response to the heelstick procedure in a cohort of newborns that we have recently studied. Our goals are to illustrate the usefulness of our reactivity framework in understanding the phenomenon of early behavioral distress, to determine if there are any perinatal factors that influence individual differences, and finally, to determine whether early differences in reactivity are related to the subsequent health of the infant.

Newborn Reactivity

To identify stable measures of reactivity, we observed 110 neonates in the newborn nursery of our affiliated teaching hospital. The sample was split nearly even by sex, with 53 males (48 percent) and 57 females (52 percent). They averaged 3,476 grams (SD = 540 g) at birth and had mean Apgar scores of 8.57 and 9.06 at one and five minutes, respectively. Mothers averaged twenty-nine years of age (range of seventeen to forty-four years). Eighty-five of the newborns (77 percent) were delivered without complications through a vertex presentation; the remaining 25 via cesarean section. Fifty-five percent of the infants were first-borns and 75 percent of their mothers indicated they would be breast-feeding (82 of 110).

In the morning of the day before discharge, when the newborns were approximately two days old, their responses to the heelstick procedure were videorecorded. The procedure required piercing each newborn's heel with a sterilized lancet. This was followed by repeated squeezing of the newborn's foot until a sufficient amount of blood was expressed. Although a number of different hospital technicians administered the heelstick over the course of our observations, the majority of instances (72 percent) were carried out by one individual. The observer noted and coded on the videotape each time the infant's foot was squeezed in order to monitor the baby's responses to the initial lance was well as to the subsequent foot squeezes. The interval between the initial heelstick and the first foot-squeeze was approximately ten seconds, with a similar duration between the perturbations that followed. Counting the initial lancing as the first perturbation, the typical neonate experienced on the order of twelve more perturbations during the procedure.

Measures of Stress. Following data collection, each newborn's reactions to the initial heelstick and to the subsequent perturbation intervals were rated on a four-point intensity scale. Vocalization was rated on a 0-to-3 scale: 3, crying (continuous rolling cry); 2, fussing (interval crying with long pauses between cries); 1, minimal vocalizing (discrete squeaks or frets); and 0, no vocalization. Facial response was coded in a similar fashion: 3, full distress (brows, cheeks, and mouth grimacing); 2, partial distress (two among brows, cheeks, or mouth grimacing); 1, minimal movement (one among brows, cheeks, or mouth grimacing); and 0, no facial response.

The highest observed intensities of vocal fussing and of facial grimacing within each interval were scored separately, interval by interval. The same rater evaluated all of the infants and her partner coded every eighth newborn for interrater reliability purposes. Agreement averaged 85 percent for the newborns rated by each observer for the vocal responses, and 75 percent for the facial responses. Observer agreement was calculated by dividing the number of intervals coded identically by the total number of intervals coded.

Overall Reactivity. Because the correlation between facial and vocal responses was high, we combined the vocal and facial intensity scores. As a consequence the combined score could range from 0 to 6. Here we first looked at the temporal course of reactivity to perturbation. Figure 1 displays the time course of the mean behavioral response for the entire sample, interval by interval. Since some subjects had the necessary blood drawn faster than others, the number of intervals varied for each infant. The data cited in the following discussion are based on the responses of 101 neonates, since 9 newborns were crying during baseline and were not included in the analyses.

As displayed in Figure 1, prior to their heels being lanced (the prestick condition), newborns were observed in a baseline state of 1.44 (SD = 1.56). In the interval immediately following the heelstick, the average intensity score (vocal plus facial response) jumped to 4.66 (SD = 1.60), clearly indicating a high initial reactivity to the procedure. A classic response decrement curve is observed across intervals 2 through 6, with intensity scores steadily dropping from 3.98 (SD = 2.06) to 2.77 (SD = 2.12). By the sixth interval (fifth foot-squeeze), the sample consists of 91 neonates for whom the perturbations continued.

Figure 1 also indicates that after five perturbations beyond the heelstick, the group of newborns as a whole exhibited an increase in reactivity. Indeed, the intensity score for interval 7 is 3.39 (SD = 2.08), with the subsequent scores all in excess of the lowest level reached in interval 6. This reactivation response, though clearly discernible, must be tempered with the fact that the intensity scores are sequentially based on fewer and fewer cases (that is, N's of 87, 77, 65, 55, 46, 34, 27, 18, and 17, for

Figure 1. Mean Reactivity Over Successive Perturbations

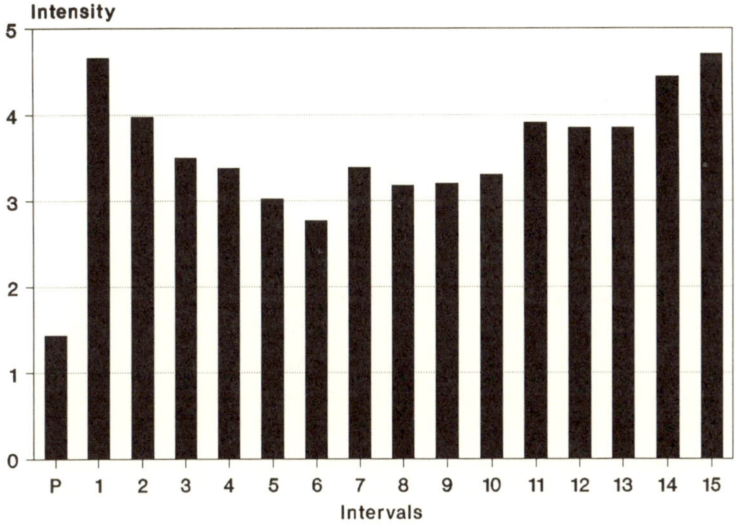

Note: P = prestick condition.

intervals 7 through 15, respectively). Hence, while continued perturbations seem to have pushed the neonates who had previously dampened into reactivations of their distressed responses, the physiology of the infants who necessitated additional foot squeezes to draw sufficient blood must be considered.

Different Measures of Reactivity. While individual intervals represent one way to characterize infants' response to perturbations, it also is possible to obtain overall measures of reactivity. Three summary measures of reactivity were computed for both the vocal and the facial measures: *initial* reaction, or the intensity score for the initial interval following the heelstick; *average* reaction, or the mean intensity level across the entire procedure; and *latency until quieting*. We found that the intensities of the vocal responses were strongly related to the facial responses for all three summary measures (r's > .50, p's < .0001). Given this correspondence between vocal distress and facial grimacing, the vocal and facial responses were summed as before to decrease the number of measures but increase the variance of the reactivity responses.

We were interested in examining the association between these three measures of reactivity in order to ascertain whether they represented different and independent types of reactions to stress. There was a significant relation between the initial response and the average overall reaction to the ensuring perturbations (r = .65; p < .0001). However, the initial reaction was not related to the latency-to-quiet measure. Newborns who initially responded with high reactivity were likely to sustain a high reaction throughout the successive perturbations, but the initial response could not predict how long it would take the newborns to quiet down. While all three measures show some relation, initial response and latency to quiet clearly were independent and represent different measures of reactivity.

Our observation of these infants at two months of age provided even stronger evidence of this independence. For forty of these babies, we observed reactions to their first inoculation. As with the measures of stress in response to a heelstick, visual and facial responses were strongly correlated, again warranting the creation of summary variables by collapsing across modalities. Consistent with the data reported for two-day-olds, the initial response was not significantly associated with the latency-to-quiet measure (Worobey and Lewis, 1989).

This parallel finding that initial response and latency to quiet were unrelated at both two days of age and two months of age supports our belief that these responses represent two different types of reactivity to a perturbation (Lewis, in press). Thus, we observed infants who had low thresholds but quieted quickly, as well as infants with low thresholds who took longer to quiet down. Moreover, some infants with high thresholds remained upset once they started to cry and continued to be upset over a long period. Creating a taxonomy of these four possibilities and determining the differential effects of threshold versus dampening remains an interesting question for further study. The use of such a taxonomy allows us to consider the two measures at once, an advantage when trying to characterize infants.

Stability of Reactivity Across Time

Clearly, newborn infants differ in their reactivity to a physical perturbation such as the heelstick procedure. Do these differences represent some momentary state difference, or are they related to some traitlike variable or disposition? A demonstration of stability across age would provide data on this question, since stability suggests that these individual differences reflect some dispositional factor. In fact, the association that we found between the reactivity measures at two days of age and at two months of age did show stability, both for the initial reactions and for the latency-to-quiet measures (Worobey and Lewis, 1989). Such findings appear to support the view that individual differences in response to perturbations reflect individual dispositional styles of reactivity.

The association across time, while significant, does not account for much of the variance. For example, the correlation for initial response over time was .37. While supportive, the order of magnitude of association suggests that other factors affect stability—in particular, the environment.

This problem was explored further by looking at the pattern of stability across the two age points. Subjects at two days of age were divided into two groups of reactors based on their initial responses. The high reactors were those subjects who showed maximum initial responses to the heelstick, while the moderate-to-low reactors were those subjects who showed less than the maximum initial responses. At two months of age these children were observed again while receiving a noxious procedure, that is, an inoculation. Of the twenty-one high responders at birth, eighteen remained high (86 percent), whereas only ten (53 percent) of the nineteen moderate-to-low responders at birth remained in this category. Such findings indicate that there is greater constancy for some ranges of initial response than for others. In summary, highly reactive infants are more likely to remain so, independent of their experiences over the two-month period. This is not so for the low-reactive infants. One likely hypothesis is that environmental experiences over the two-month period affect low-reactive infants more than high-reactive infants.

Such findings give rise to a general proposition about the dispositional factors of reactivity, their stability, and the effects of the environment. It seems reasonable to suggest that for certain levels of reactivity, individual differences seen either at or soon after birth are likely to be maintained, independently of the nature of the environment; while at other levels of reactivity, individual differences are likely to be highly affected by the nature of the environment. When applied to our data, this theory suggests that infants who are highly reactive remain so whether or not their environments are responsive to their needs. Low-to-moderate reactive infants, on the other hand, are highly affected by their environments. For these infants, a responsive environment would result in low-to-moderate reactivity, whereas a less responsive environment would result in high reactivity, thus accounting for the lack of stability over time.

We have found that stability appears greater for highly reactive infants than for low-to-moderate reactive infants. The reverse may be true in some cases. For example, are there low-reactive or "easy" babies who remain easy no matter what their environments, and "difficult" babies who are highly affected by their environments? While the particulars may vary, the general proposition appears worthy of further test: the interaction of environment and disposition is unlikely to be the same across all levels of individual differences.

Prenatal Characteristics and the Reactivity Response

The heelstick data support the view that individual differences in reactivity appear at or soon after birth. Moreover, these differences show varying degrees of stability, at least across the first two months of life. The source or sources of these differences is difficult to determine. On the one hand, the differences may be owing to genetic factors, or they may be owing to a variety of prenatal factors, including such variables as the toxicity of the fetal environment or the nutritional level of the mother. Other factors might include the nature or the difficulty of the delivery or the condition of the child at birth, as indicated in such measures as birth weight or Apgar score.

In order to explore the possible effect of prenatal factors on the neonatal stress response, we obtained data on each infant's sex, birth order, method of delivery (cesarean section versus normal), birth weight, Apgar score at one and five minutes, and mother's age. These variables were related to the infants' three reactivity measures: initial response, mean response, and latency to quiet.

We first examined the effects of each of these perinatal variables separately on neonatal reactivity at two days of age. There were no significant effects of the sex of the child, mode of delivery, mother's age, or Apgar score at one minute. Birth order, birth weight, and Apgar score at five minutes, however, do appear to affect infant reactivity. In general, the reactivity measure most affected was latency to quiet. First-born infants took longer to quiet down than latter-borns (M = 143.1 secs versus 81.1 secs, respectively; $p < .01$). Likewise, infants with high Apgar scores and heavier birth weights took longer to quiet down than infants with lower Apgar scores and lighter birth weights.

Having looked at each variable separately, we next attempted to predict the three different neonatal reactivity responses by utilizing all the variables at the same time. Sex, birth order, mode of delivery, birth weight, Apgar score at one and five minutes, and mother's age were all entered together into a least-square regression equation in order to predict either initial response or latency to quiet. No combination of these variables predicted initial response; however, latency to quiet was predicted by them (multiple $r = .39$, $r^2 = .15$, $p < .06$). Birth weight and birth order contributed most significantly to this regression, with Apgar score just failing to reach significance.

These findings together appear to indicate that healthy infants are more likely to cry longer than less healthy infants at birth. Although not significant, healthy infants, at least at two days of age, also were more likely to have higher initial responses. This is consistent with the view that robust crying is a sign of a healthy newborn (Als, 1982; Lester, 1985).

Reactivity and Health

The psychological and medical literature is replete with examples of stressful life events, life styles, and personality attributes that affect subsequent health outcomes in the adult population (see Dorian and Garfinkel, 1987, for a review). This increasingly large corpus of research, which includes many epidemiological studies of humans and a significant number of experiments with animals, suggests a major role for psychological factors both in the etiology of some diseases and in the severity of symptoms in others.

One of the early studies demonstrated a relation between personality characteristics of the individual and rate of recovery from infectious mononucleosis (Greenfield, Roessler, and Rosley, 1959). Such factors as high motivation, overactive fathers, and poor academic performance have been found to significantly increase the risk of the clinical expression of infectious mononucleosis (Kasl, Evans, and Niederman, 1979). Numerous researchers have demonstrated the link between the quantity and magnitude of stressful events and subsequent illness (Holmes and Masuda, 1974). Many psychological factors have emerged as influences on the capacity of stressors to affect health in animals and humans. These factors include the ability of the organism to control the stressor, the amount of feedback the organism receives, and whether the stressor is predictable (Levine, 1983). Although there is an extensive literature on stress, coping, and disease with human adults and animals as subjects, to our knowledge no studies have extended this work to explore these related phenomena with human infants.

We looked at the forty infants for whom we had data on reactivity to the perturbation of the heelstick procedure, as well as on their responses to inoculation at two months of age, in order to see the relation between early responses to stress and health outcomes. When these infants were eighteen to twenty-four months old, their mothers were sent a health questionnaire in which they were asked to indicate the illnesses that the infants had had over the preceding year.

In order to explore this problem, we looked at birth characteristics (that is, birth weight and Apgar score), reactivity to heelstick at two days of age, and reactivity to inoculation at two months of age. The reactivity measure used was the latency-to-quiet measure, although mean reactivity gave similar results. A path-analytic model was constructed with total number of illnesses at eighteen to twenty-four months of age as the outcome measure. Figure 2 presents this path analysis. Observe first the birth variables. Birth weight, but not Apgar, is positively related to reactivity at two days. Children with high birth weights take longer to quiet down than children with lower birth weights. Notice, however, that neither birth weight nor Apgar is itself related to children's reactivity at two months of age, nor are they related to total illness at two years of age. Reactivity at two days was significantly related to reactivity at two months. The children who took comparatively longer to cry at two days were likely also to have taken longer to cry at two months.

Of particular importance is the finding that reactivity at two days of age was negatively related to total illness at eighteen to twenty-four

**Figure 2. Path Analysis of Early Responses
to Stress and Health Outcomes**

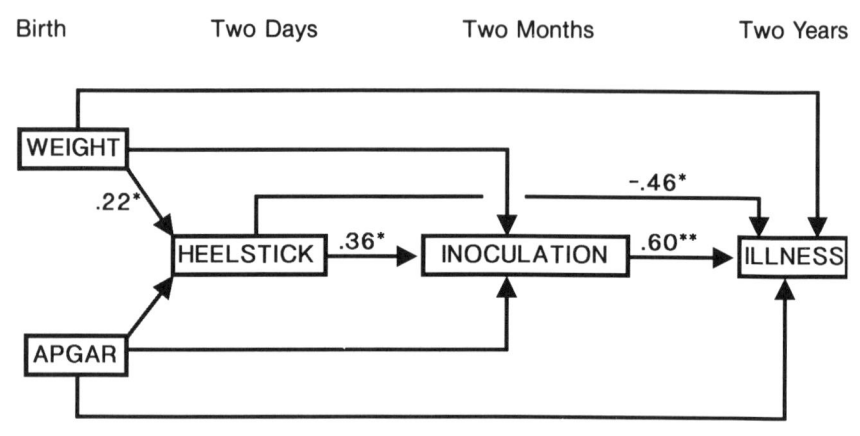

Birth   Two Days   Two Months   Two Years

```
WEIGHT ─────────────────────────────────────────┐
       ╲                        -.46*           │
        .22*  ┌──────────────────────────┐      │
         ╲    │                          ▼      ▼
        HEELSTICK ──.36*──▶ INOCULATION ──.60**──▶ ILLNESS
         ╱                     ▲
APGAR ──┘──────────────────────┘
```

Note: Latency to quiet used to measure response to heelstick and inoculation perturbations.
*$p < .05$.
**$p < .01$.

months of age ($\beta = -.46$). We can understand these findings if we recall that the highly reactive newborns are the healthier infants. Thus, children who are more reactive at two days (a measure of health and vigor) have less illness at eighteen months. This is consistent with reports by others (Lind and others, 1970; Michaelsson and Sirvio, 1976). The relation is quite different for reactivity at two months. Infants who are most reactive at two months, that is, are less able to cope with stress, are more likely to have a greater history of illness a year or more later.

This model indicates several important factors related to development, response to a stressor, and health. The first finding is that healthy children are more likely than less healthy children to be highly reactive to stress in the newborn period. This is because the newborn child does not yet have available highly developed, sophisticated mechanisms to cope with stress (Gunnar, Malone, and Fisch, 1985), and one would expect high reactivity to be associated with bigger and more robust children (Lester and Zeskind, 1978).

Individual differences in reactivity to stress when infants become older reflect differences in ability to organize and control stressful events (Prechtl, 1984). As the infants mature, we would expect that those who are better at coping with stress should show less reactivity to stressors; for example, they should quiet down faster. Thus, although high reactivity at first may be a sign of health, as infants mature it becomes a sign of potential difficulty. This developmental function in the child's ability to cope with stress explains why reactivity in the newborn is negatively related to health, whereas reactivity in the two-month-old infant is positively related to health.

Finally, these results have important implications for the relation between ability to cope with stress and subsequent illness. We have been able to demonstrate that infants who show more stress to a perturbation at two months are those infants who are more likely to have more illnesses at eighteen to twenty-four months. Clearly, further research with large samples is necessary in order to confirm this relation. Nevertheless, these results are consistent with a vast literature on human adults and animals that demonstrates the interaction between ability to cope with stress and illness (Holmes and Masuda, 1974).

Individual Differences in Reactivity: Disposition, Trait, or Process

We have explored individual differences in reactivity to stress and have looked at some of the antecedent conditions that might account for individual responses to stress in the newborn period, how these individual differences in response are consistent over time (at least over the first few months of life), and how these differences are related to health outcomes. The data only in part support a notion of a disposition or trait. Our findings suggest that individual differences seen in the first two days of life also are manifest at two months of life, especially for those infants who show high reactivity. The data do not support consistency over time for infants with moderate-to-low reactivity. Thus, any trait model or notion of disposition must be limited. Indeed, the research literature on traits or dispositions clearly suggests that consistency, a sine qua non of trait theory, cannot easily be located (Mischel, 1977). Children differ in their reactivity and differ over time as a function of both individual differences in temperament as well as socialization practices. The data from a variety of sources indicate that mothers and fathers respond differently to infant distress (Worobey, Laub, and Schilmoeller, 1983) and that differential responses have powerful effects on how children learn to organize and cope with stressful events.

It should be noted in this regard that Lewis (in press) has reported on group differences in responses to inoculation. He looked at a group of three- to five-month-old Japanese and American infants when they were being inoculated. The findings from this study confirm earlier anthropological reports that infants show vast differences in their responses to perturbations as a function of group membership (Caudill and Frost, 1973; Freedman and Freedman, 1969). American children, on the one hand, cried and showed upset at three to five months of age, while the Japanese children showed no crying and very little facial and vocal upset. A variety of possibilities may explain these findings; however, the socialization differences between Japanese and American children must figure prominently in any explanation (Caudill and Weinstein, 1969). Japanese children for the first three years are in constant contact with their mothers. Their mothers carry them around and sleep in the same bed with them. This is very different from the socialization practices experienced by most American children. Such differences may well account for group as well as individual differences in responses to stress. Consider that when Japanese infants must signal distress, they need simply grunt or move, since they are within close proximity to their mothers. American children, on the other hand, often placed at far distances from their caregivers, need to cry loudly to get attention.

Conclusion

Findings reported here should not be construed as only supporting a traitlike characteristic. Rather, the model we propose is an interactive one in which characteristics of the individual are shaped by perinatal factors. In turn, characteristics of individuals affect environments, changing the environment and at the same time changing the individual. This complex interactive process between children's endogenous characteristics and their interaction with the exogenous variables of environment creates individual differences that can be observed at any moment in time. That these individual differences, at one moment in time, may affect subsequent characteristics of the individual, for example, health status, cannot be construed as a dispositional characteristic. Rather, once again, the characteristics of the child in interaction with the environment, over the twelve months between our observations of stress and our measures of health, need to be considered.

References

Als, H. "Toward a Synactive Theory of Development: Promise for the Assessment and Support of Infant Individuality." *Infant Mental Health Journal*, 1982, *3*, 229-243.

Anand, K.J.S., and Hickey, P. R. "Pain and Its Effects in the Human Neonate and Fetus." *New England Journal of Medicine*, 1987, *317*, 1321-1329.

Anders, T. F., Sachar, E. J., Kream, J., Roffwarg, H. P., and Hellman, L. "Behavioral State and Plasma Cortisol Response in the Human Newborn." *Pediatrics*, 1970, *46*, 532-537.

Bates, J. E. "Temperament in Infancy." In J. D. Osofsky (ed.), *Handbook of Infant Development.* (2nd ed.) New York: Wiley, 1987.

Birns, B., Barten, S., and Bridger, W. H. "Individual Differences in Temperament Characteristics of Infants." *Transactions of the New York Academy of Sciences*, 1969, *31*, 1071-1083.

Brazelton, T. B. *Neonatal Behavioral Assessment Scale.* (2nd ed.) Clinics in Developmental Medicine, no. 88. Philadelphia: Lippincott, 1984.

Buss, A. H., and Plomin, R. *Temperament: Early Developing Personality Traits.* Hillsdale, N.J.: Erlbaum, 1984.

Caudill, W., and Frost, L. "A Comparison of Maternal Care and Infant Behavior in Japanese Families." In W. P. Lebra (ed.), *Youth Socialization and Mental Health: Mental Health Research in Asia and the Pacific.* Vol. 3. Honolulu: The University of Hawaii Press, 1973.

Caudill, W., and Weinstein, H. "Maternal Care and Infant Behavior in Japan and America." *Psychiatry,* 1969, *323,* 32-43.

Craig, K. D., McMahon, R. J., Morison, J. D., and Zaskow, C. "Developmental Changes in Infant Pain Expression During Immunization Injections." *Social Science and Medicine,* 1984, *19,* 1331-1337.

D'Apolito, K. "The Neonate's Response to Pain." *American Journal of Maternal Child Nursing,* 1984, *9,* 256-258.

Dorian, B., and Garfinkel, P. E. "Stress, Immunity, and Illness—A Review." *Psychological Medicine,* 1987, *17,* 393-407.

Field, T. M., and Goldson, E. "Pacifying Effects of Nonnutritive Sucking on Term and Preterm Neonates During Heelstick Procedures." *Pediatrics,* 1984, *74,* 1012-1015.

Franck, L. S. "A New Method to Quantitatively Describe Pain Behavior in Infants." *Nursing Research,* 1986, *35,* 28-31.

Freedman, D. G., and Freedman, N. "Behavioral Differences Between Chinese-American and American Newborns." *Nature,* 1969, 224-227.

Goldsmith, H. H., Buss, A. H., Plomin, R., Rothbart, M. K., Thomas, A., Chess, S., Hinde, R. A., and McCall, R. B. "Roundtable: What Is Temperament? Four Approaches." *Child Development,* 1987, *58,* 505-529.

Goldsmith, H. H., and Campos, J. J. "Fundamental Issues in the Study of Early Temperament: The Denver Twin Temperament Study." In M. E. Lamb and A. L. Brown (eds.), *Advances in Developmental Psychology.* Hillsdale, N.J.: Erlbaum, 1986.

Greenfield, N. S., Roessler, R., and Rosley, A. P. "Ego Strength and Length of Recovery from Infectious Mononucleosis." *Journal of Nervous and Mental Diseases,* 1959, *128,* 125-128.

Grunau, R.V.E., and Craig, K. D. "Pain Expression in Neonates: Facial Action and Cry." *Pain,* 1987, *28,* 395-410.

Gunnar, M., Malone, S., and Fisch, R. "The Psychobiology of Stress and Coping in the Human Neonate: Studies of Adrenocortical Activity in Response to Aversive Stimulation." In T. M. Field, P. M. McCabe, and N. Schneiderman (eds.), *Stress and Coping.* Hillsdale, N.J.: Erlbaum, 1985.

Gunnar, M., Malone, S., Vance, G., and Fisch, R. "Coping with Aversive Stimulation in the Neonatal Period: Quiet Sleep and Plasma Cortisol During Recovery from Circumcision in Newborns." *Child Development,* 1985, *56,* 824-834.

Holmes, T. H., and Masuda, M. "Life Changes and Illness Susceptibility." In B. S. Dohrenwend and B. P. Dohrenwend (eds.), *Stressful Life Events: Their Nature and Effects.* New York: Wiley, 1974.

Izard, C. E., Hembree, E. A., Dougherty, L. M., and Spizzirri, C. C. "Changes in Facial Expression of 2- to 19-Month-Old Infants Following Acute Pain." *Developmental Psychology,* 1983, *19,* 418-426.

Izard, C. E., Hembree, E. A., and Huebner, R. R. "Infants' Emotion Expressions to Acute Pain: Developmental Change and Stability in Individual Differences." *Developmental Psychology,* 1987, *23,* 105-113.

Kasl, S. V., Evans, A. S., and Niederman, J. C. "Psychosocial Risk Factors in the Development of Infectious Mononucleosis." *Psychosomatic Medicine,* 1979, *41,* 445-466.

Lester, B. M. "Introduction: There's More to Crying than Meets the Ear." In B. M. Lester and C. F. Boukydis (eds.), *Infant Crying: Theoretical and Research Perspectives*. New York: Plenum, 1985.

Lester, B. M., and Zeskind, P. S. "Brazelton Scale and Physical Size Correlates of Neonatal Cry Features." *Infant Behavior and Development*, 1978, *1*, 393-402.

Levine, S. "A Psychobiological Approach to the Ontogeny of Coping." In N. Garmezy and M. Rutter (eds.), *Stress, Coping, and Development in Children*. New York: McGraw-Hill, 1983.

Lewis, M. "Culture and Biology: The Role of Temperament." In R. Barr and P. Zelazo (eds.), *Challenges to Developmental Paradigms*. Hillsdale, N.J.: Erlbaum, in press.

Lewis, M., and Thomas, D. "Cortisol Release in Infants Response to Stress and Inoculation." *Child Development*, in press.

Lind, J., Vuoreukoski, V., Rosberg, G., Parkaneu, T. J., and Wasz-Hockert, O. "Spectrographic Analysis of Vocal Response to Pain Stimuli in Infants with Down's Syndrome." *Developmental Medicine and Child Neurology*, 1970, *12*, 478-486.

Lipsitt, L. P. "Stress in Infancy: Toward Understanding the Origins of Coping Behavior." In N. Garmezy and M. Rutter (eds.), *Stress, Coping, and Development in Children*. New York: McGraw-Hill, 1983.

Michaelsson, K., and Sirvio, P. "Cry Analysis in Congenital Hypothyroidism." *Folio Phoniatrica*, 1976, *26*, 40-47.

Mischel, W. "The Interaction of Person and Situation." In D. Magnussan and N. S. Endler (eds.), *Personality at the Crossroads: Current Issues in Interactional Psychology*. Hillsdale, N.J.: Erlbaum, 1977.

Prechtl, H. F. "Epilogue." In H. F. Prechtl (ed.), *Continuity of Neural Functions from Prenatal to Postnatal Life*. London: Blackwell Scientific, 1984.

Riese, M. L. "Assessment of Behavioral Patterns in Neonates." *Infant Behavior and Development*, 1983, *6*, 241-246.

Rothbart, M. K., and Derryberry, D. "Development of Individual Differences in Temperament." In M. E. Lamb and A. L. Brown (eds.), *Advances in Developmental Psychology*. Vol. 1. Hillsdale, N.J.: Erlbaum, 1981.

Tennes, K., and Carter, D. "Plasma Cortisol Levels and Behavioral States in Early Infancy." *Psychosomatic Medicine*, 1973, *35*, 121-128.

Thomas, A., and Chess, S. *Temperament and Development*. New York: Brunner/Mazel, 1977.

Worobey, J., Laub, K. W., and Schilmoeller, G. L. "Maternal and Paternal Responses to Infant Distress." *Merrill-Palmer Quarterly*, 1983, *29*, 33-45.

Worobey, J., and Lewis, M. "Individual Differences in the Reactivity of Young Infants." *Developmental Psychology*, 1989, *25*, 663-667.

Michael Lewis is professor and chief of the Institute for the Study of Child Development, Robert Wood Johnson Medical School, University of Medicine and Dentistry of New Jersey.

John Worobey is associate professor of human development in the Department of Nutritional Sciences, Cook College/NJAES, Rutgers University.

David Thomas is assistant professor of pediatrics at Robert Wood Johnson Medical School, University of Medicine and Dentistry of New Jersey.

Temperamentally based individual differences in infant response to frustrating situations have important implications for subsequent response to challenge and help in understanding patterns of social interaction in older children.

Infant Response to Frustrating and Mildly Stressful Events: A Positive Look at Anger in the First Year

Nathan A. Fox

Psychologists often get into trouble when they attempt to define a concept that has broad and wide-ranging meaning with the popular culture. Stress (the noun or the verb) is a good example of this semantic quandary. Scientific research on stress has included studies of life-threatening events and their contribution to disease (Dohrenwend, 1975), competitive situations that elevate blood pressure and lead to cardiovascular problems (Dembroski, MacDougall, Herd, and Shields, 1979), and surgical procedures that cause changes in the neuroendocrine system (Gunnar, Malone, Vance, and Fisch, 1985). The range of elicitors of stress is large and most probably dependent on contextual factors. So too, it may be dangerous to use any single physiological or behavioral measure as an indicator of stress since most physiological responses are complex and multiply determined. For example, the secretion of cortisol in response to an elicitor was one viewed as an indication that the animal or subject had undergone stress (Levine and Coe, 1985). However, researchers found that cortisol could be elevated in response to many different novel events. Animals that are fed a diet of laboratory chow and then given a fresh vegetable for the first time exhibit a dramatic rise in cortisol. Thus, to some extent, the concept of stress has become an all-purpose category that may have little scientific value or psychological significance.

The research in this chapter was supported in part by a grant from the National Institutes of Health (HD #17899).

Research on infancy has also contributed to the confusion of definition given the variety of stressors and stressful experiences that affect young children. Studies of response to surgery (circumcision) and to maternal separation are two examples of extremes of stressful situations in which physiological responses have been measured (Gunnar, Malone, Vance, and Fisch, 1985; Porter, Porges, and Marshall, 1988; Reite and others, 1978). Both elicitors have been called stressors and both produce stress responses in infants. Clearly, however, they are very different in the immediate and long-term physiological and behavioral responses that they stimulate.

As a consequence of these differences in effects, it is important at the outset to define exactly what parameters of stress are being discussed and where these fit into the larger framework of stress research. The stress or stressor discussed in this chapter is known as a frustrating event. The frustration is in response to the prevented attainment of a desired goal. For example, being given a cookie and then having it taken away might be construed as a frustrating event. Being presented with an attractive toy that is then placed in a clear container, visible but unobtainable, might be a frustrating event. Similarly, being placed in an infant seat and having one's arms held down in place could also be defined as a frustrating event. Each of these conditions is frustrating because in each instance the subject is prevented from attaining a desired goal (the cookie, the attractive toy, freedom of movement). The use of frustration as an example of a stressor is in line with the general stress literature (Levine and Coe, 1985). There is recent work on the contribution of daily life hassles to cardiovascular disease. The typical stress questionnaire lists a number of frustrating events as part of the inventory (being stuck in traffic is a good example).

The subject's response to frustration, the manner in which the infant or adult copes with frustration, is of obvious interest. Successful coping with the daily frustrations of everyday life can affect a subject's health (Lazarus and Folkman, 1984). But how do infants cope with frustration and is there meaning to individual differences in their responses? Little is known about infant coping in relation to frustration.

In this chapter I argue that there are important individual differences in infant responses to frustrating situations. These different patterns of behavior have important implications for subsequent responses to challenge. I also argue that these different coping responses are in part temperamentally based and that these individual differences in temperament help us understand patterns of social interaction exhibited by older children.

Research on Frustrating Situations with Infants

Developmental psychologists have been placing their subjects in frustrating situations for some time. Bruner (1969) was interested in the development of guided reaching in infancy and devised a situation in which infants had to retrieve a toy from behind a see-through Plexiglas barrier. This work achieved detailed descriptions of the phases through which the infants passed in their attempts to solve the problem of retrieving the object. But little attention was paid to the affective responses of the infants when they did not have the skills to correctly solve the puzzle. Similarly, Diamond (1988) developed a task in which infants attempted to retrieve an attractive toy from underneath a Plexiglas box with just one open side. Diamond described the phases of competence of the infants but there is little data on the affective responses of infants who were frustrated by the task.

In another type of frustrating experience, Provost and Gouin-Decarie (1979) were interested in the elicitation of anger in young infants. To accomplish this goal, they had mothers hold their infants' hands down on a table for a set period of time. The authors note that in response to this restraint infants displayed a good deal of anger. Stenberg, Campos, and Emde (1983) elicited anger in seven-month-olds by repeatedly offering and then taking away a biscuit from each infant.

Across these different studies there is substantial variability in the responses of infants to these frustrating situations. In part this variability may be the result of different measurement systems. Some studies used heart rate responses (Provost and Gouin-Decarie, 1979), and others used precise measurement of facial movements (Stenberg, Campos, and Emde, 1983). But another source of variability may be the infant's temperament. Early in life infants may exhibit stable dispositions that characterize their response to frustration.

Infant response to frustration has been recognized recently as an important temperamental difference (Rothbart, 1981). Rothbart included the dimension of distress in response to limitations as one of six temperamental variables in infancy. She defined this dimension as the child's response to waiting for food, refusing food, being in a confined place or position, being dressed or undressed, or being prevented access to an object to which the child is attending. Parents rate their infants' responses to these frustrating situations. A high score represents a child who exhibits distress or negative affect during these conditions.

Other temperament researchers have used the expression persistence of goal orientation to describe a subset of these behaviors. Torgensen and Kringlen (1978), for example, and Goldsmith and Gottesman (1981) both present data on the heritability of this dimension in infants. In general, there are a number of theorists that view infant response to frustration as an individual difference with a hereditary constitutional basis.

While the variation in distress responses to limitations during the first year clearly includes negative reactions to frustration, there is an expectation, within Rothbart's theory at least, of a diminution of reactions with age. As the child matures, reactivity, including responses to frustration, is modulated. The child develops strategies for self-regulation of emotional arousal. Rothbart argues (Posner and Rothbart, 1980; Rothbart and Posner, 1985) that the infant's developing ability to attend selectively to stimuli in the environment permits multiple strategies for dealing with physiological arousal. That arousal in turn is a function, early in life, of the intensity of the stimulus and, later on, a function of the appraisal process (with reduction of arousal accompanying successful assimilation of novelty and continued arousal associated with unsuccessful assimilation). In other words, given stimuli of moderate uncertainty or novelty, there will be individual differences in infant reaction to the stimulus and individual differences in modulation of that reaction. The latter differences are in part a function of regulatory strategies available to the child.

Reactivity and Self-Regulation: Their Relation to Infant Temperament

We have applied Rothbart's model of change in infant reactivity to the problem of understanding both infant response to frustration and its relation to subsequent social behavior. In particular, we have investigated whether there are stable individual differences in infant response to frustration, whether these differences are related to socioemotional behavior during the second year of life, and whether these individual differences in reactivity have a physiological basis.

Rothbart (Rothbart and Derryberry, 1981) identifies two central dimensions of temperament: reactivity and regulation. Reactivity involves specific parameters of the organism's responses to different levels of stimulation. This dimension is measured with variables such as latency, threshold, and intensity of response. Self-regulation involves the organism's attempts to deal with stimulation and the modulation of the reactive responses. This dimension is measured by the organism's success in inhibiting arousal.

Rothbart's model can be reorganized into a two-by-two table that shows the interaction of the dimensions of reactivity and regulation (see Table 1). We have speculated about the different personality types that might fall within each of the four quadrants of this table. For example, individuals who are highly reactive but are able to modulate their reactivity might be characterized as expressive of their emotions, sociable, and uninhibited; whereas those who are highly reactive but are unable to regulate their responses might be characterized as uncontrollable or hyperactive. Inhibited or highly controlled and nonexpressive individuals might be those whose threshold to respond is high but, once aroused, are highly regulative of their behavior; whereas depressed and socially withdrawn individuals might be low in both reactivity and regulation.

We have used this conceptual framework, in our research program, as a heuristic for studying variations in the temperamental dimensions of reactivity and regulation. Obviously both reactivity and regulation are continua along which individual variation is distributed. However, examination of the extreme cases of the quadrants described in Table 1 may be helpful in understanding the complex physiological-behavioral linkages within these two dimensions (Fox, 1989; Kagan, Reznick, and Snidman, 1987).

There are four qualifiers to our model that are useful in developing testable hypotheses. The first deals with the measurement of reactivity and regulation. Neither need be considered solely from a behavioral standpoint. Physiological responses, such as heart rate or heart rate variability, can serve as indices of reactivity or regulation and demonstrate within-subject stability across conditions. For example, some children may display a high and stable heart rate at rest. This pattern may continue across stimulus conditions designed to elicit wariness, even though behavioral responses may not necessarily be consistent across stimulus conditions. It may therefore be a useful strategy to partition subjects by their physiological responses and examine differences in overt behavior.

The second qualifier is that the contexts and specific measures used as indices of reactivity are important in understanding differences in this dimension. The same stimulus may elicit a positive or a negative response, or no response at all, depending on the context in which it is presented. In addition, there is in all probability response fractionation rather than response regimentation. That is, differences in reactivity may not change in the same direction or even over the same time period. For example, a subject may display no overt behavior, a sudden transient heart rate change, and subsequently a large change in cortisol concentration in response to a novel event. Thus measures of reactivity must be used with these considerations in mind.

Table 1. Interaction of Infant Reactivity and Regulation

Reactivity	Regulation High	Regulation Low
High	Expressive Sociable Uninhibited	Uncontrollable Hyperactive
Low	Nonexpressive Inhibited Highly controlled	Depressed Socially withdrawn

Source: Adapted from Rothbart and Derryberry, 1981.

The third qualifier is that the concepts we are dealing with change with maturation. There are important changes in the extent to which physiology influences behavior and is a stable, individual characteristic across age. For example, there are well-documented differences at birth in the level of heart rate variability among normal healthy infants (Lewis, Wilson, Ban, and Baumel, 1970; Porges, 1974: Stifter and Fox, in press). These differences are not very stable during the initial half of the first year, although within-subject stability increases during the second half of the first year of life (Fox, 1989). The lack of stability and predictability from the newborn period and the increasing stability during the latter part of the first year may indicate that physiological-behavioral relations increasingly become synchronized with development. Heart rate variability in the newborn period may reflect general behavioral organization (DiPietro, Larson, and Porges, 1987), and with development it may come to reflect more specific, organized behavioral responses (Fox, 1989).

The fourth qualifier is that the physiological mechanisms influencing reactivity and regulation may not be identical. Recent data suggest that differences in reactivity are present early on in the first year but that regulation of reactivity develops more slowly. Regulation of emotional distress seems to emerge during the second year of life and may involve the development of certain cognitive abilities (Kopp, 1982; Posner and Rothbart, 1980).

Psychophysiology of Reactivity: A Brief Review

The idea that differences in reactivity or tolerance to frustration may have a physiological basis is the product of two bodies of literature. The first is the search for relations between autonomic patterning and individual differences in personality. This literature, beginning with Eppinger and Hess (1915), indicates that individuals might differ in the degree to which the various branches of their autonomic nervous systems dominate or regulate behavior. Individuals with low resting-levels of heart rate and high heart-rate variability, both of which reflect parasympathetic dominance, were considered vagotonic. These individuals have been described as depressed, listless, and unreactive. Individuals with high resting-levels of heart rate and low heart-rate variability have been characterized as sympathetically dominant (sympatheticotonia), high strung, and highly reactive. Wenger (1941) proposed a balance theory with five different types of autonomic nervous system response patterns. Each type was associated with a particular pattern of reactivity.

Lacey and Lacey (1958) reported the serendipitous finding of different patterns of baseline skin conductance variability. These patterns were subsequently related to performance on a reaction time task. And Porges (1976) has speculated that individual variations in parasympathetic balance may be related to differences in reactivity. In this model, individuals with attentional problems, or those who could not make use of attentional strategies to regulate behavioral activity, were characterized as being low in parasympathetic influence. In contrast, individuals who were unable to shift attention were placed on the opposite end of the parasympathetic continuum.

There is also an experimental literature relating individual differences in autonomic patterning to behavioral reactivity. Porges (1972), for example, found that, with adults, the greater the level of resting vagal tone, the fewer the errors on a reaction time task. Linnemeyer and Porges (1986) found that nine-month-old infants with high vagal tone were more likely to exhibit a novelty preference on a visual attention task than infants with lower vagal tone. Richards (1985, 1987) found that infants with a high level of resting respiratory sinus arrhythmia were less distracted and exhibited greater sustained attention to novelty than infants with a lower level of arrhythmia. They also exhibited greater heart rate deceleration to novel stimuli. And, DiPietro, Larson, and Porges (1987) found that infants with high vagal tone who were breast-fed were more reactive on the Neonatal Behavioral Assessment Scale (Brazelton, 1973) than those with lower vagal tone.

In our own work, described below, we view differences in vagal influence as reflections of two different levels of behavioral control. Individual differences in vagal tone during the neonatal and early infancy period are seen to reflect general behavioral organization and reactivity to the environment: high vagal influence reflects better organization and increased reactivity in comparison to lower vagal influence. With development, vagal control assumes a specific role in the mediation of attentional responses that are involved in reaction to novelty and in regulation of reactive behavior. Recent work by Richards (1987) illustrates the changes in influence of respiratory sinus arrhythmia over the first year and the increasing relation between this individual difference and sustained attention. Theoretically, then, we would expect individual differences in vagal tone to be associated with reactivity to novel and mildly stressful events and, increasingly with age, to reflect differences in attentional style and regulation.

Methodological Issues in the Measurement of Autonomic Patterning

The heart period process is a complex result of neural and extraneural (for example, thermoregulatory, blood pressure) influences (Porges, 1986). Respiratory sinus arrhythmia is the extractable component in the pattern of heart rate attributable to parasympathetic influence (Katonah and Jih, 1975). This arrhythmia was first observed in EKG tracing as the rhythmic change synchronized with breathing. Heart rate increases with inspiration and decreases with expiration. This pattern has been studied by a number of researchers as a marker of individual differences in susceptibility to stress and attentional style (Grossman, 1983). Porges, McCabe, and Yongue (1982) have demonstrated that the amplitude of respiratory sinus arrhythmia is primarily the result of parasympathetic or vagal influence on the heart.

The vagal tone statistic is the variance in heart period attributable to respiration. The higher the number, the greater the power in the respiratory frequency of the heart period process. We have investigated the stability of vagal tone across the first year of life (Fox, 1989; Stifter and Fox, in press) and over a six-month period with preschool-age children (Fox and Field, in press). Data on the repeated measurement of heart period, heart period variance, and vagal tone over the first year of life indicated little stability between the newborn period and the later age points of five and fourteen months, but moderate stability onward beginning at five months of age. In addition, test-retest correlations across a six-month interval for these measures in a sample of preschool children were quite high (.70 to .90). Thus, from at least the middle of the first year, there is some stability of individual differences in vagal tone.

The choice of measurement for vagal tone is quite important. Researchers who study differences in respiratory sinus arrhythmia have sometimes used the peak-to-trough height of the respiratory cycle (Grossman and Wienthes, 1986) rather than examine rhythmicity within the heart period process. This technique, while adequate for certain studies of adult populations in which movement is kept to a minimum, may not be adequate for studies with infants and young children. Researchers who study infant and child populations have traditionally used different measures of the variance in heart period to approximate the contribution of respiratory sinus arrhythmia in the heart period process. Included among these measures are the variance of the process or of the range (Garcia-Coll, Kagan, and Reznick, 1984) and the mean of the absolute value of the successive differences (Fox, 1983). Each of these measures indirectly taps a portion of the variance in the heart period attributable to respiration. A number of more recent techniques have employed spectral analysis (Richards, 1987) and digital filtering (Porges, 1986) to extract the variance owing to respiratory sinus arrhythmia. Richards focuses on a measure called the extent of respiratory sinus arrhythmia (Harper and others, 1976), while Porges calls his measure V (an estimate of vagal tone).

Research on Autonomic Patterning and Reactivity in Infancy

We have been studying the relations between vagal tone and reactivity in infants over a number of years. Our first set of studies examined reactivity during social interaction, and we chose facial expression as the measure of reactivity. We were interested in finding out if there were differences in infant facial expressivity that related to autonomic patterning. In an initial study Fox and Gelles (1984) found a positive association between heart rate variability and facial expression in three-month-old infants. Infants with high tonic heart-rate variability displayed more facial expressions than infants with low tonic heart-rate variability. Following this finding, Stifter, Fox, and Porges (1989) found that tonic vagal tone was associated with facial expressivity. Five-month-old infants with high tonic vagal tone displayed more positive and negative facial expressions than five-month-old infants with low vagal tone. Note that in both studies vagal tone was associated with facial expressions of both positive and negative affect. This is important since the hypothesized relation between vagal influence and motor arousal is not necessarily valence related.

We next turned our attention to individual differences in infant responses to frustration and their possible physiological bases. In order to examine the origins and physiological correlates of this reactivity, we conducted a longitudinal study with a sample of middle-class families from the Washington, D.C., metropolitan area. Families were recruited when mothers and infants were in the newborn nursery at a local hospital. While each infant was still in the nursery, EKG was recorded during both active and quiet sleep. Also, when each infant was in a quiet, alert state, a pacifier withdrawal task was administered. This task, modeled after Bell, Weller, and Waldrop (1971), involved having the infant first suck on a pacifier and then abruptly removing it from the infant's mouth. The infant's latency to cry to pacifier withdrawal was recorded.

The infants were first seen in our laboratory at five months of age. At that time we recorded infant EKG while each child sat quietly on the mother's lap. Among the conditions that were administered to the infant was the moderate restraint task that Provost and Gouin-Decarie (1979) used in their research on elicitation of anger and frustration. This task involved having the child's mother hold her infant's hands down by the side of the infant seat for a period of time up to two minutes in duration. We coded the infants' facial and vocal expressions as well as motor behavior during these periods. The infants were again seen at fourteen months of age. At this time, EKG was again recorded. EKG was recorded in seven different instances. The first recording was a two-minute baseline period. This was followed by presentation of a two-minute segment of "Sesame Street," during which heart rate was recorded for a second two-minute baseline period. This was followed by presentation of one novel object for two minutes and then six novel objects for two minutes. During each of these periods, heart rate was recorded. Finally, at the end of the experimental session, heart rate was recorded during a third two-minute baseline period and a second two-minute segment of "Sesame Street." Each infant was then observed in a free-play situation and in a situation of presentation of an unfamiliar adult. The adult first entered and sat down on the floor in a corner of the room with head bowed. This lasted for two minutes or ended if the child approached and attempted to interact with the adult. After the two-minute period, the adult began to play with a toy. Again, if the child initiated interaction, the adult played with the child. Finally, if the child had still not approached after this two-minute period, the unfamiliar adult attempted to engage the child in play.

Our interest in the study was to examine the pattern of autonomic balance and its relation to behavior. As a first step we selected infants from both extremes of balance, those with high parasympathetic tone and those with low tone. In order to identify these infants, we computed their vagal tone scores at fourteen months of age from the EKG recordings and selected only those infants whose seven independent recordings were either all above the mean or else all below the mean in score. Thirty-one subjects were identified in this manner out of the total sixty infants in the sample. Figure 1 presents the mean vagal tone scores for the two groups for each of the seven recording conditions.

The subsequent analyses involved these thirty-one infants. We examined, in turn, the data on newborns, five-month-olds, and fourteen-month-olds as a function of the two extremes in parasympathetic tone. Of the thirty-one infants in these analyses, data were available on thirty subjects for the pacifier withdrawal procedure: seventeen cried and thirteen did not cry. There were no associations between heart rate variability group at fourteen months of age and response to pacifier withdrawal. There were also no differences in any of the newborn autonomic measures between infants who cried and those who did not cry in response to pacifier withdrawal. The correlation between vagal tone at the neonatal period versus at the fourteen-month-old period was negligible (.01).

The data on moderate physical restraint at five months of age were somewhat more revealing. Data were available on twenty-nine of the thirty-two subjects tested at this age. Twelve infants cried to moderate restraint and seventeen did not cry. Infants who cried in response to arm restraint at five months of age displayed greater vagal tone [$F(1, 22) = 7.44$, $p < .01$] than those who did not cry (see Table 2). The comparison for heart period was near significance [$F(1, 22) = 3.93$, $p < .06$], indicating that infants who cried in response to arm restraint tended to have slower heart rates than those who did not cry. Table 2 presents the means and standard deviations for these measures.

Within-age correlations between the five-month-olds' autonomic measures and the summary measures of reactivity and regulation revealed that infants with high vagal tone displayed more negative reactivity [$r(24) = .39$, $p < .03$] and a tendency toward greater positive reactivity at five months of age [$r(24) = .32$, $p < .06$] than infants with low vagal tone. In addition, there was a positive relationship between heart period

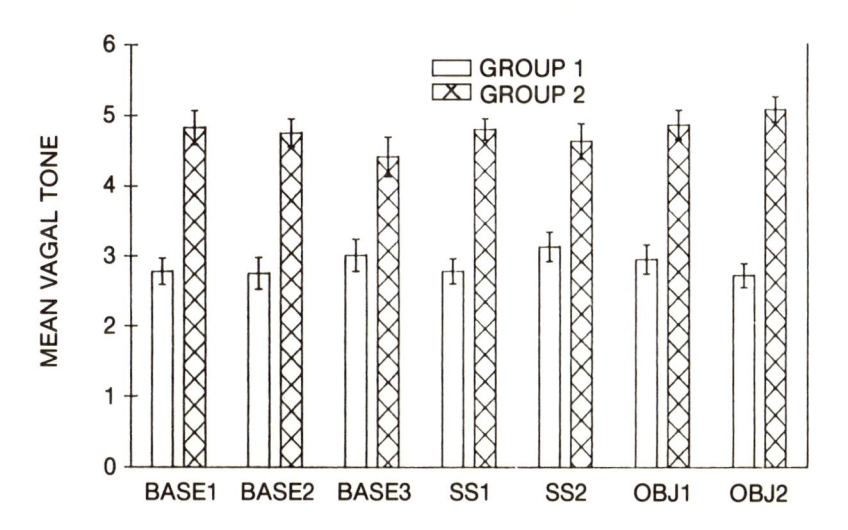

Figure 1. Mean Vagal Tone Scores of Fourteen-Month-Olds

Note: Group 1 (*N* = 15) is infants with high parasympathetic tone; group 2 (*N* = 16) is infants with low parasympathetic tone.
BASE1 is the first two-minute baseline.
BASE2 is the two-minute baseline prior to object manipulation.
BASE3 is the final two-minute period after the experimental session.
SS1 is the two-minute period viewing "Sesame Street" after BASE1.
SS2 is the two-minute period viewing "Sesame Street" after BASE3.
OBJ1 is the two-minute period while subjects manipulated one novel object.
OBJ2 is the two-minute period while subjects manipulated six objects.

variability and regulation within the group of infants who cried in response to arm restraint. Infants with high heart period and heart period variability, compared to those with low levels, displayed greater regulation of distress. There were no significant associations between newborn autonomic measures and five-month positive or negative reactivity or regulation.

Examination of the relation between newborns' reactivity to pacifier withdrawal and five-month-olds' responses to moderate restraint revealed that ten of the twelve infants who cried at moderate restraint also cried in response to pacifier withdrawal. Ten of the seventeen infants who did not cry at moderate restraint also did not cry in response to pacifier withdrawal. The relationship between responses to arm restraint and group membership at fourteen months of age was significant. Of the twelve criers among five-month-olds, nine were in the low and variable heart rate group, while thirteen of the seventeen noncriers were in the high and stable group at fourteen months of age [χ^2 (1) = 5.59, $p < .02$].

Table 2. Heart Rate Measures for Criers and Noncriers

	Restraint	
Five-month-olds	Cried (N = 12)	Did not cry (N = 17)
Heart period	429.47	410.27
	(24.18)	(23.26)
Heart period variance	27.86	18.39[a]
	(10.39)	(6.34)
Vagal tone	3.39	2.48[a]
	(.79)	(.83)

[a] Means and standard deviations for five-month data broken up by criers and noncriers to arm restraint. Standard deviations are in parentheses.
$p < .05$.

An examination of both infant behavior and physiology at five months of age in relation to physiological reactivity grouping at fourteen months of age revealed that infants who at fourteen months displayed high vagal tone exhibited more negative reactivity [$F (1, 27) = 4.39$, $p < .05$] at five months than infants who at fourteen months displayed low vagal tone. In addition, there were significant group (fourteen-months group) differences in heart period at five months [$F (1, 23) = 4.33$, $p < .05$] and vagal tone at five months [$F (1, 23) = 12.10$, $p < .002$]. Infants with high vagal tone at fourteen months had lower heart rate (high heart period) and higher vagal tone at five months than infants who had low vagal tone at fourteen months. Table 3 presents the means and standard deviations of these data. The data from the assessment at five months of age indicate that there is a relation between autonomic balance, specifically parasympathetic tone, and both positive and negative reactivity at five months. Infants with high vagal tone are more reactive than infants with lower vagal tone. Infants who cried at moderate restraint displayed greater vagal tone at five months and at fourteen months of age than infants who did not cry. There also seems to be some stability across the nine-month period from five to fourteen months of age. Infants at five months with high vagal tone continue to exhibit this pattern at fourteen months.

The data on fourteen-month-olds provide an interesting insight into the relation between infant reactivity to frustration during the first year and subsequent social behavior. Results of the data analysis revealed that infants at fourteen months with high vagal tone exhibited a significantly shorter latency to approach the stranger than infants with low vagal tone [$F (1, 29) = 9.73$, $p < .004$].

In an effort to closely examine the pattern of behavior of the two groups of infants in response to the stranger, their behavior was divided

Table 3. Temperament and Heart Rate Measures Divided by Fourteen-Month Vagal Tone

Five-month-olds	Fourteen-month-olds Low vagal tone (N = 16)	Fourteen-month-olds High vagal tone (N = 15)
Positive reactivity	24.78 (15.24)	26.18 (13.97)
Negative reactivity	25.87 (44.56)	61.73[a] (47.32)
Heart period	410.38 (23.76)	429.76[a] (22.83)
Heart period variance	19.62 (6.64)	26.51 (10.98)
Vagal tone	2.40 (.69)	3.45[a] (.79)

[a] Means and standard deviations for five-month data broken up by high and low vagal tone groups at fourteen months. Standard deviations are in parentheses.
$p < .05$.

into three categories: those who approached within the first three-minute period (when the stranger had her head down and was not interacting); those who approached during the second, four-minute period (when the stranger attempted to initiate interaction); and those who did not approach at all during the seven-minute period. Table 4 presents the distribution of subjects by group for these three approach categories. As indicated, the difference between groups is between those infants who approached prior to the stranger's overtures (eleven of fifteen in the high vagal tone group) and those who subsequently approached when the stranger attempted interaction (ten of sixteen in the low vagal tone group). The chi-square value for this table is significant $[\chi^2 (2) = 13.72, p < .001]$. There was also a tendency for infants with high vagal tone to show a shorter latency of approach to the toy robot than infants in the low vagal tone group $[F (1, 29) = 2.65, p < .10]$. Eight of fifteen children in the group with high vagal tone approached the robot, whereas only three of sixteen in the low vagal tone group approached at all. There were no significant differences in latency to cry at maternal separation between the two groups, although here again infants with high vagal tone showed a shorter latency to begin crying than exhibited by infants with low vagal tone. This pattern of findings suggests that infants with high vagal tone at fourteen months of age are more likely to approach either an unfamiliar adult or a novel object than fourteen-month-olds with low vagal tone.

Table 4. Latency of Approach to Stranger by Fourteen-Month-Olds

Vagal Tone Group	1–3 Min	3–7 Min	No Approach
Low	2	10	4
High	11	1	3

Note: Figures are number of infants in each vagal tone group, as distributed by latency of approach in a free-play situation.

The data also indicate stability of the autonomic/behavior relations across age. Compared to the infants with low vagal tone at five months of age, infants with high vagal tone at five months displayed a shorter latency to approach the unfamiliar adult [r (25) = -.42, $p < .02$] and a shorter latency to cry at maternal separation at fourteen months [r (25) = -.43, $p < .02$]. Interestingly, the newborn autonomic data predicted little about subsequent social behavior at fourteen months of age. The only discernible relationship between newborns' behavior and fourteen-month-olds' behavior involves response to pacifier withdrawal and response to maternal separation. Newborns who cried at pacifier withdrawal displayed shorter latencies to cry at maternal separation when fourteen months old than displayed by infants who did not respond to pacifier withdrawal in their newborn period [F (1, 28) = 4.96, $p < .03$].

These data are interesting for two reasons. First, they indicate that there is a positive relationship between vagal tone and reactivity during early infancy. Infants with high vagal tone were more reactive than infants with lower vagal tone, particularly in response to frustrating situations. This finding seems congruent with our other data on facial expressivity and with data from other studies on attention and irritability. The indication is that differences in vagal tone reflect variations in reactivity. The second point of interest is in the relationship between reactivity to frustration during the first year of life and social behavior during the second year. Originally, we had expected that more reactive infants would be more inhibited and withdrawn in their social interactions. Contrary to these expectations, the more reactive children were the more social children at fourteen months.

It is important to frame these findings in terms of the measures of reactivity used for the assessment at five months. The test administered was moderate restraint of the hands, and the measures of reactivity were the frequency, duration, and intensity of anger and frustration expressed during the restraint. In other words, infants who were more reactive during this test were expressing more anger and frustration at the situation.

Reactivity to frustration, whether the result of abruptly withdrawing a pacifier or of restraining movement, may be quite different from reactivity to painful stimuli or to novel, nonfrustrating events. These latter events (such as inoculation) may tap sensory or physiological threshold differences between subjects, whereas the response to frustration may tap infant evaluation of context and differences in intrinsic motivation. For example, data available on response to inoculation (Izard, Hembree, and Huebner, 1987) indicate that in early infancy the response is expression of distress, whereas in older age groups the response is expression of anger. The distress response may be genetically and physiologically based, whereas the later, anger response may be a result of the infant's developing ability to interpret the context and attempt to avoid the situation.

In their paper on anger expressions in infancy, Stenberg, Campos, and Emde (1983) found that the magnitude of the anger response in seven-month-olds was influenced by whether mothers or a stranger initiated the trials (taking a biscuit away from each infant). If the stranger initiated the first trial, the anger was greater when the mother initiated the next trial than when mothers initiated the first trial. Infants were displaying more anger toward their mothers than toward strangers after being involved in a frustrating situation with these adults. Stenberg, Campos, and Emde (1983) reasoned that infants may have expected their mothers to comfort them and end the frustration rather than prolong it. Hence the increased anger toward mother in the second trial.

Infant response to frustration thus may be an important window on individual differences in infant-coping style and anger expression. And these differences may reflect differences in intrinsic motivation with respect to blocking of goal-oriented behavior rather than simply physiological thresholds of response to sensory stimuli (Izard, 1977).

In our data we found that reactive infants developed into sociable toddlers. What seemed to emerge during the second half of the first year was an increase in reflective approach responses, coupled with an ability to regulate arousal. This ability allowed each infant to respond positively to novel, mildly stressful events.

To the extent that infant behavior in response to frustration reflects coping with blocked, goal-oriented behavior, it is not surprising to find that differences in coping style are ultimately related to social behavior. Infants who have learned or are temperamentally predisposed to search and explore novel situations are likely to be frustrated by events that block these goals. And, it is not unreasonable that these same infants will tend to be sociable and interactive. These infants seem to view novelty as a challenge and not as a stressor because they have at their disposal coping strategies that regulate their reactive responses.

At a physiological level, differences in vagal tone between infants may reflect heightened response to sensory stimulation during early infancy. With maturation there may be increased inhibition of this reactivity via increases in sustained attention. Physiological differences may predispose some infants to easily develop strategies for modulating their physiological reactivity and hence allow them wide range in exploring novel events and situations.

References

Bell, R. Q., Weller, G. M., and Waldrop, M. F. *Newborn and Preschool: Organization of Behavior and Relations Between Periods.* Monograph of the Society for Research in Child Development, no. 36 (serial no. 142). Chicago: Society for Research in Child Development, 1971.

Brazelton, T. B. *Neonatal Behavioral Assessment Scale.* Philadelphia: Lippincott, 1973.

Bruner, J. S. "Eye, Hand, and Mind." In D. Elkind and J. H. Flavell (eds.), *Studies in Cognitive Development: Essays in Honor of Jean Piaget.* New York: Oxford Press, 1969.

Dembroski, T. M., MacDougall, J. M., Herd, J. A., and Shields, J. L. "Effects of Level of Challenge on Pressor and Heart Rate Responses in Type A and B Subjects." *Journal of Applied Social Psychology,* 1979, *9,* 209-228.

Diamond, A. "Retrieval of an Object from an Open Box: The Development of Visual-Tactile Control of Reaching in the First Year of Life." Unpublished paper, University of Pennsylvania, 1988.

DiPietro, J. A., Larson, S. K., and Porges, S. W. "Behavioral and Heart Rate Pattern Differences Between Breast- and Bottle-Fed Neonates." *Developmental Psychology,* 1987, *23,* 467-474.

Dohrenwend, B. P. "Sociocultural and Socio-Psychological Factors in the Genesis of Mental Disorder." *Journal of Health and Social Behavior,* 1975, *16,* 365-392.

Eppinger, H., and Hess, L. "Vagotonia: A Clinical Study in Vegetative Neurology." *Journal of Nervous and Mental Disease,* 1915, *20,* 1-93.

Fox, N. A. "Maturation of Autonomic Control in Preterm Infants." *Developmental Psychobiology,* 1983, *16,* 495-504.

Fox, N. A. "Psychophysiological Correlates of Emotional Reactivity During the First Year of Life." *Developmental Psychology,* 1989, *25,* 364-372.

Fox, N. A., and Field, T. "Young Children's Responses to Entry into Preschool: Psychophysiological and Behavioral Findings." *Journal of Applied Developmental Psychology,* in press.

Fox, N., and Gelles, M. "Face-to-Face Interaction in Term and Preterm Infants." *Infant Mental Health Journal,* 1984, *5,* 192-205.

Garcia-Coll, C., Kagan, J., and Reznick, J. S. "Behavioral Inhibition in Young Children." *Child Development,* 1984, *56,* 28-37.

Goldsmith, H. H., and Gottesman, I. I. "Origins of Variation in Behavioral Style: A Longitudinal Study of Temperament in Twins." *Child Development,* 1981, *52,* 91-103.

Grossman, P. "Respiration, Stress, and Cardiovascular Function." *Psychophysiology,* 1983, *20,* 284-300.

Grossman, P., and Wienthes, K. "Respiratory Sinus Arrhythmia and Parasympathetic Cardiac Control: Some Basic Issues Concerning Quantification, Application, and Implications." In P. Grossman, K. H. Janssen, and D. Vaitl (eds.), *Cardiorespiratory and Cardiosomatic Psychophysiology.* New York: Plenum, 1986.

Gunnar, M. R., Malone, S., Vance, G., and Fisch, R. O. "Coping with Aversive Stimulation in the Neonatal Period: Quiet Sleep and Plasma Cortisol Levels During Recovery from Circumcision in Newborns." *Child Development,* 1985, *56,* 824-834.

Harper, R. M., Hoppenbrouwers, T., Sterman, M. B., McGinty, D. J., and Hodgman, J. "Polygraphic Studies of Normal Infants During the First Six Months of Life. Part I: Heart Rate and Variability as a Function of State." *Pediatric Research*, 1976, *10*, 945-951.

Izard, C. E. *Human Emotions*. New York: Plenum, 1977.

Izard, C. E., Hembree, E. A., and Huebner, R. R. "Infants' Emotion Expressions to Acute Pain: Developmental Change and Stability in Individual Differences." *Developmental Psychology*, 1987, *23*, 105-113.

Kagan, J., Reznick, J. S., and Snidman, N. "The Physiology and Psychology of Behavioral Inhibition in Children." *Child Development*, 1987, *58*, 1459-1473.

Katona, P. G., and Jih, F. "Respiratory Sinus Arrhythmia: Non-Invasive Measure of Parasympathetic Cardiac Control." *Journal of Applied Physiology*, 1975, *39*, 801-805.

Kopp, C. B. "Antecedents of Self-Regulation: A Developmental Perspective." *Developmental Psychology*, 1982, *18*, 199-214.

Lacey, J. I., and Lacey, B. C. "The Relationship of Resting Autonomic Activity to Motor Impulsivity." *Research Publications Association for Research in Nervous and Mental Disease*, 1958, *36*, 144-209.

Lazarus, R., and Folkman, S. *Stress, Appraisal, and Coping*. New York: Springer, 1984.

Levine, S., and Coe, C. L. "The Use and Abuse of Cortisol as a Measure of Stress." In T. Field, P. McCabe, and N. Schneiderman (eds.), *Stress and Coping*. Vol. 1. Hillsdale, N.J.: Erlbaum, 1985.

Lewis, M., Wilson, C. D., Ban, P., and Baumel, M. H. "An Exploratory Study of Resting Cardiac Rate and Variability from the Last Trimester of Prenatal Life Through the First Year of Postnatal Life." *Child Development*, 1970, *41*, 799-812.

Linnemeyer, S. A., and Porges, S. W. "Recognition Memory and Cardiac Vagal Tone in Six-Month-Old Infants." *Infant Behavior and Development*, 1986, *9*, 43-56.

Porges, S. W. "Heart Rate Variability and Deceleration as Indexes of Reaction Time." *Journal of Experimental Psychology*, 1972, *92*, 103-110.

Porges, S. W. "Heart Rate Indices of Newborn Attentional Responsivity." *Merrill-Palmer Quarterly*, 1974, *20*, 131-154.

Porges, S. W. "Peripheral and Neurochemical Parallels of Psychopathology: A Psychophysiological Model Relating Autonomic Imbalance to Hyperactivity, Psychopathy, and Autism." In H. Reese (ed.), *Advances in Child Development*. Vol. 11. New York: Academic Press, 1976.

Porges, S. W. "Respiratory Sinus Arrhythmia: Physiological Basis, Quantitative Methods, and Clinical Implications." In P. Grossman, K. Janssen, and D. Vaitl (eds.), *Cardiac Respiratory and Somatic Psychophysiology*. New York: Guilford, 1986.

Porges, S. W., McCabe, P. M., and Yongue, B. G. "Respiratory-Heart Rate Interactions: Physiological Implications for Pathophysiology and Behavior." In J. Cacioppo and R. Petty (eds.), *Perspectives in Cardiovascular Psychophysiology*. New York: Guilford, 1982.

Porter, F. L., Porges, S. W., and Marshall, R. E. "Newborn Cries and Vagal Tone: Parallel Changes in Response to Circumcision." *Child Development*, 1988, *59*, 495-505.

Posner, M. I., and Rothbart, M. K. "The Development of Attentional Mechanisms." *Nebraska Symposium on Motivation*, 1980, *28*, 1-52.

Provost, M. A., and Gouin-Decarie, T. "Heart Rate Reactivity of Nine- and

Twelve-Month-Old Infants Showing Specific Emotions in a Natural Setting." *International Journal of Behavioral Development,* 1979, *2,* 109-120.

Reite, M., Short, R., Kaufman, I. C., Stynes, A. J., and Pauley, J. D. "Heart Rate and Body Temperature in Separated Monkey Infants." *Biological Psychiatry,* 1978, *13,* 91-105.

Richards, J. E. "Respiratory Sinus Arrhythmia Predicts Heart Rate and Visual Responses During Visual Attention in 14- and 20-Week-Old Infants." *Psychophysiology,* 1985, *22,* 101-109.

Richards, J. E. "Infant Visual Sustained Attention and Respiratory Sinus Arrhythmia." *Child Development,* 1987, *58,* 488-496.

Rothbart, M. K. "Measurement of Temperament in Infancy." *Child Development,* 1981, *52,* 569-578.

Rothbart, M. K., and Derryberry, D. "Development of Individual Differences in Temperament." In M. E. Lamb and A. L. Brown (eds.), *Advances in Developmental Psychology.* Vol. 1. Hillsdale, N.J.: Erlbaum, 1981.

Rothbart, M. K., and Posner, M. I. "Temperament and the Development of Self-Regulation." In C. L. Hartledge and C. R. Telzrow (eds.), *The Neuropsychology of Individual Differences: A Developmental Perspective.* New York: Plenum, 1985.

Stenberg, C. R., Campos, J. J., and Emde, R. N. "The Facial Expression of Anger in Seven-Month-Old Infants." *Child Development,* 1983, *54,* 178-184.

Stifter, C. A., and Fox, N. A. "Infant Reactivity and Regulation: Physiological Correlates of Newborn and Five-Month Temperament." *Developmental Psychology,* in press.

Stifter, C. A., Fox, N. A., and Porges, S. W. "Facial Expressivity and Vagal Tone in Five- and Ten-Month-Old Infants." *Infant Behavior and Development,* 1989, *12,* 127-137.

Torgensen, A. E., and Kringlen, E. "Genetic Aspects of Temperament Differences in Infants." *Journal of the American Academy of Child Psychiatry,* 1978, *17,* 443-449.

Wenger, M. A. "The Measurement of Individual Differences in Autonomic Balance." *Psychosomatic Medicine,* 1941, *3,* 427-434.

Nathan A. Fox is professor of human development at the Institute for Child Study, University of Maryland, College Park.

Traumatic events early in life can not only cause acute alterations in immune responses but also derail the normal developmental trajectory of certain immunological processes.

Immunological Consequences of Maternal Separation in Infant Primates

Christopher L. Coe, Gabriele Lubach, William B. Ershler

Our current views on attachment and infant development have been strongly affected by a fertile exchange of ideas between the fields of comparative and developmental psychology. At least since the 1950s, biological and evolutionary considerations have been readily accepted and incorporated as explanatory principles in developmental papers. One of the best examples of this profitable cross-fertilization was the heavy reliance of John Bowlby on animal research, especially the primate studies of Harry Harlow, when he formulated his ideas on attachment and loss (Bowlby, 1973). Animal research has continued to play an important role in stimulating new ideas about many developmental topics, ranging from sex differences in behavior to the effects of child abuse and the physiological basis of childhood psychopathology. This type of animal

---

This research was supported in part by National Institute of Mental Health Grant MH41659 (CLC), Office of Naval Research Contract N00014-87-0227 (CLC, WBE), and National Science Foundation grant BNS-871430 (GL). CLC receives partial salary support from the Wisconsin Regional Primate Center (P51 R000167-27), and WBE has a Veterans Administration Merit Award. We would also like to acknowledge H. Crispen for help in sample collection and graph preparation and O. Ramos for assistance with the immune assays. Several of the early studies were conducted in collaboration with S. Levine and L. Rosenberg (Stanford University). This chapter is listed as Publication No. 29-006 of the Wisconsin Regional Primate Center.

research is well known and is often categorized under the heading of developmental psychobiology.

Less well known are parallel studies that have emanated from another discipline, psychoneuroimmunology. During the past two decades, it has become increasingly apparent that psychological variables can influence a number of basic immune responses, and that this relationship may account for some of the effects of stressful life events on disease susceptibility (Ader, 1981). While the effect of stress on immunity may be observed at any point in the life span, it is the thesis of this chapter that the developing organism is particularly vulnerable. This vulnerability stems both from the infant's strong emotional reactions to challenge as well as from the lability of its endocrine and immune responses. In our research on the effects of psychological disturbance on endocrine and immune responses, we have consistently found that young primates show larger and more prolonged physiological reactions than adults. Moreover, the perturbations may ultimately have more long-lasting consequences in the young organism because several physiological systems are still undergoing significant maturational changes. Although the primate infant is immunologically competent at birth, the immune system undergoes many important changes during the postnatal period prior to puberty (Cauchi, 1981). Thus, traumatic events early in life can not only cause acute alterations in immune responses but also derail the normal developmental trajectory of certain immunological processes. This chapter reviews many examples of transient changes in immune responses, all of which we have observed during periods of psychological disturbance. In addition, we provide some evidence that early rearing events can exert a lingering effect on certain immune responses in the primate infant.

As alluded to in the first paragraph, our studies are based on extensive research demonstrating that the monkey infant is a suitable model for investigating the biology of attachment and maternal separation (Reite and Field, 1985). We know, for example, that the primate infant, like the human neonate, is born with a strong predisposition to form an attachment bond with a caregiving figure. At birth, the infant is attracted toward any object, animate or inanimate, that fulfills its innate needs for oral and tactile gratification (Harlow and Zimmermann, 1959). However, within the first few days of life, the bonding process becomes selective, and the particular object of attachment becomes imbued with affect. As the bond becomes more focused and solidified, the infant shows an increasingly strong reaction to involuntary separation from the attachment object. Much of our research has been concerned with the physiological consequences of this separation response. In addition, we have been investigating the possible immunological consequences of deviations from the normal rearing environment. That is, to what extent is the healthy maturation of the endocrine and immune systems tied to the typical maternal rearing process? We know that the nursery-reared monkey will show extensive behavioral pathology, and there is some evidence of alterations in its endocrine and neural activity (Champoux and others, in press; Kraemer, Ebert, Schmidt, and McKinney, in press; Martin, Sackett, Gunderson, and Goodlin-Jones, 1988; Sackett and others, 1973). Our research has begun to show that there are also some long-term immunological effects of nursery rearing and of early weaning from the mother.

Numerous studies have been conducted to describe the course of the separation response in young monkeys, and many investigators have remarked on the similarities in the response of children and nonhuman primates to maternal loss (Mineka and Suomi, 1978). In particular, there are many analogous features during the "protest" phase, which involves a period of agitated behavior and vocalization in primate infants. The subsequent phase, often described as the depressive or "despair" stage, is more variable and depends on the separation environment and the infant's previous experiences. Our first studies were designed to document any changes in immune responses during the first week after maternal separation. However, we also took advantage of the variation in separation responses across different environments to simultaneously evaluate the capacity of certain psychological variables to ameliorate the separation reaction and its physiological sequelae. We were especially interested in determining whether separation from the mother in a familiar setting would have a smaller effect on immune responses than a separation in an unfamiliar setting. Similarly, we were happy to find in several studies that the presence of familiar social companions markedly reduced, or entirely eliminated, the immunological effects of maternal loss.

The finding of immunological changes in infant primates following maternal separation may not come as a surprise to those readers who are already familiar with the large literature on changes in other physiological systems after the infant is separated from the mother. In the monkey infant, at least, virtually all aspects of stress physiology become activated during the first several days after separation. Activation of the autonomic nervous system is reflected in the marked changes in heart rate, body temperature, and sleep patterns (Reite and Field, 1985). Many studies have also shown parallel activation and release of the pituitary-adrenal hormones, lasting from one to two days in most primate species and up to two weeks in the squirrel monkey (Coe, Wiener, and Levine, 1983). Increases in brain dopamine, serotonin, and norepinephrine activity also occur during the first day, and norepinephrine utilization may be increased for several days (Wiener, Bayart, Faull, and Levine, in press). Given the broad physiological actions of these hormones and neurotransmitters, it was reasonable to predict that there would be some degree of change in immune responses. Nevertheless, the first immunological studies on nonhuman primates were slow in coming, and even today, equivalent studies have not been conducted in any detail on children. Although many studies on rodents and farm animals have indicated that premature weaning from the mother could influence several immune processes (Ader, 1981; LaBarba, 1970; Kelley, 1980), it was not until 1982 that an important pilot study demonstrated a reduced ability of lymphocytes to proliferate during a two-week social separation in two monkey infants (Laudenslager, Reite, and Harbeck, 1982). In this chapter, we are able to provide a more complete description of the changes in immune responses in separated primate infants. In addition, we begin to address the important question of which psychological variables are efficacious in reducing the immunological effects of separation.

The cost and availability of nonhuman primates for research was certainly one factor that accounted for the delay in the research. However, even more important factors are the incredible complexity of the immune system and the difficult technical hurdles that must be overcome in order to make the necessary measurements. The task is much more complicated than that confronted in equivalent studies of the endocrine system because, unlike hormones that are secreted by readily discernible glands, the immune system is organized at the cellular level. There are many different types of white blood cells, as well as numerous soluble factors, that are secreted by the cells to mobilize and coordinate an integrated immune response. To assess changes in the immune system, and to draw overall conclusions about the state of an organism's immunological competence, one must attempt to monitor several different immune responses. Otherwise, there is the risk of an erroneous conclusion drawn on the basis of a change in one arm of the immune system that may not extend to another aspect of immunity.

For the reader who is unfamiliar with immunology, we digress briefly to review some important points about the immune system. The immune system has several major functions, of which the most well known is its role in protecting the individual against foreign pathogens (bacteria, viruses, and parasites) and environmental toxins. The immune system must also protect the individual against his or her own cellular mistakes and defects, ridding the body of mutagenic and virally infected cells, as well as cellular debris and tissue breakdown products. Diseases that suppress the immune system, such as AIDS, have made it extremely clear how important the maintenance of this normal immune capability is to our health and well-being. To respond to environmental challenges and to cleanse the internal milieu, a number of different cells have evolved with specialized functions. Some white blood cells, such as the eosinophil and neutrophil, have relatively primitive phagocytic functions and serve an important role in the initial containment of infection through their ability to engulf foreign substances. Other cells, such as the macrophage, have an equally important job: to recognize the presence of a foreign substance and to alert and recruit other white blood cells, especially the lymphocytes, to mount an integrated response. Once the lymphocytes have become activated, the appropriate B lymphocytes begin to proliferate and start to make antibody against the foreign substance or antigen. This antibody response is regulated, in turn, by still other lymphocytes that are derived from the thymus gland with a special ability to up- and down-regulate immune responses (that is, helper and suppressor cells). Foreign substances that become coated with antibody or other cellular products, such as complement proteins, are then removed from circulation. Macrophages are particularly important in this final effector stage, which involves degradation and elimination of the antigen.

Similar types of cells and mechanisms are involved in other immunological responses aimed against defective cells and cancerous tissue made by the host. In this case, lymphocytes derived from the thymus (cytotoxic T cells and natural killer cells) play an important role, helping to lyse and destroy the body's abnormal cells. These T lymphocytes have been of particular interest to researchers in psychoneuroimmunology because of the field's long-standing interest in the relationship between stress and cancer. T cell regulation will also be important in understanding the relationship between psychological factors and autoimmune diseases, a condition that involves erroneous attacks by the immune system on healthy cells.

Even this brief review serves to demonstrate the difficulty of the task faced by a researcher who is interested in determining the immunological consequences of a particular psychological event. A thorough evaluation must include an assessment of several different white blood cells and their respective functions (for a more detailed discussion, see Glaser and others, 1987). In addition to the question of which immune cell to study, the researcher must choose between the many different assay techniques that can be employed in this type of research. Some assays are relatively straightforward and simply involve quantifying the number of cells or the quantity of a particular immune-modulating substance, such as interferon. In addition, a wide array of in vitro assays are also available for assessing the functional activity of each type of white blood cell. These assays involve separating the particular cells from blood samples and quantifying their activity under specific test conditions. For example, the lymphocyte proliferation assay, which was used in the first primate separation study, involves stimulating cells with plant proteins (mitogens) and assessing the degree to which the cells begin to proliferate and undergo protein synthesis. An equally valid approach, and one that is becoming more popular again, involves a direct assessment of immune responses in vivo. In animal models, the host may be challenged by eliciting an antibody response to an antigen, by evoking a skin reaction to an immunogenic substance, or through assessment of the immune system's ability to contain an implanted tumor.

In our studies on immune responses in infant monkeys, we have tried to incorporate a mixed array of in vivo and in vitro measures to obtain a global assessment of their immune state. For the most part, the total pattern of change appears to make biological sense, although at this point in the research program there are still some discrepant responses that we can not fully account for. What is abundantly clear, however, is that a significant number of immunological responses are altered by a period of sustained psychological disturbances in infant monkeys.

Leukocyte Redistribution

When Hans Selye (1950) first began to describe the stress response of animals and human patients, he noted that there were decreases in the weight of the thymus gland and lymph nodes, and changes in the number of circulating white blood cells. These changes were so reliable that he incorporated them into one of three criteria of the stressed state, along with endocrine activation and gastrointestinal ulcers. The occurrence of thymolymphatic involution and lymphocytopenia provide some of the most overt evidence of the relationship between stress and immunity.

In several studies, we attempted to characterize the changes in white blood cells in peripheral blood following periods of maternal separation lasting up to seven days (Coe and Scheffler, 1989). We studied squirrel monkey infants ranging between six and twelve months of age, at a point when they are physically independent and no longer suckling but still emotionally dependent on the mother. Small blood samples (< 1 ml) were obtained before and after removal of the infant from its mother. During the separation, the infants were each housed alone in a previously unfamiliar cage. Total white blood cell counts were determined with a Coulter counter, and differential cell counts were obtained by staining blood smears with a Wright-Giemsa stain and counting the different types of cells with a light microscope.

As expected, within twenty-four hours after removal from the mother, there was a dramatic shift in the number and type of cells found in peripheral blood (Figure 1). Eosinophils were no longer seen in the blood smears. Lymphocytes, which had been the most prevalent cell type found in normal infant blood, decreased markedly. Paralleling the disappearance of these cells, there was an outpouring of neutrophils from the tissue compartment into peripheral blood, and they were now the most common cell type found in stressed samples. Although small by comparison to the changes in other cell types, there was also modest decrease in the number of blood monocytes found in separated infants.

Figure 1. Cell Patterns in Undisturbed Versus Maternally Separated Squirrel Monkey Infants

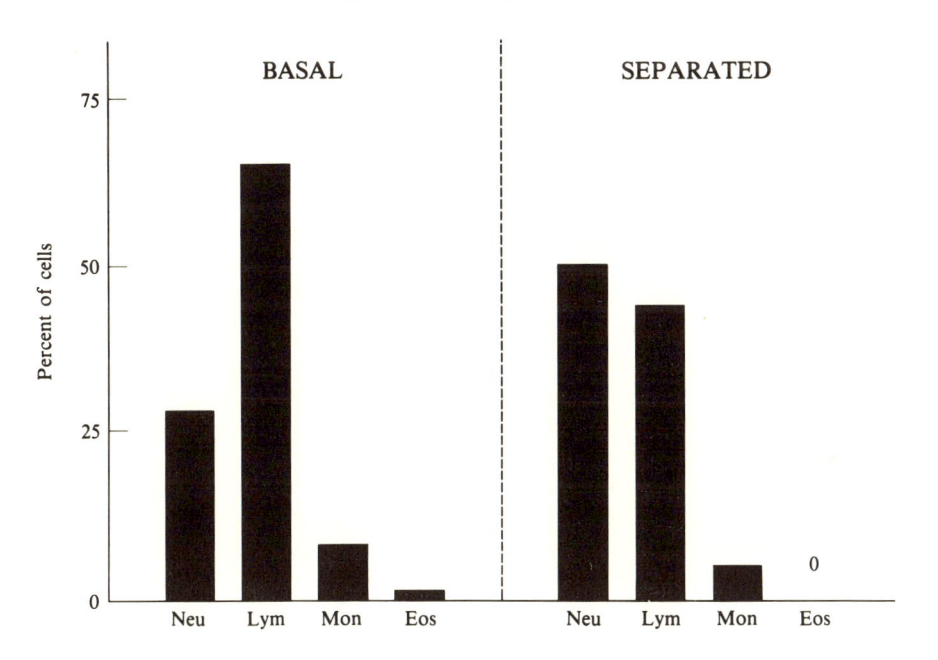

Note: Blood samples obtained before and twenty-four hours after removal from mothers. $N = 5$; Neu = neutrophils; Lym = lymphocytes; Mon = monocytes; Eos = eosinophils.
Source: Coe and Scheffler, 1989.

The initial shift in the lymphocyte/neutrophil ratio reflects an important aspect of the stress response that is often overlooked. It has often been assumed all stress-induced changes are bad, including the change in cell traffic, because of the erroneous belief that all of the disappearing lymphocytes are destroyed. In actuality, the initial response may be biologically beneficial because many of the lymphocytes are temporarily relocated into bone marrow and lymph nodes. Thus, the redistribution locates lymphocytes in the lymph nodes, where they can encounter foreign antigens, and in bone marrow, where they stimulate the production of new lymphocytes (Cohen and Crnic, 1984). Simultaneously, neutrophils, which are normally sequestered in tissue, move out to the periphery where they could help in the initial containment of infection.

However, the beneficial reaction ultimately becomes maladaptive when the cell redistribution is sustained over many hours and days, and the lymphocytopenia involves significant cell loss. At this point, it may be associated with an inhibition of many immune responses. In a study of twelve infant squirrel monkeys, we found that there was a 50 percent reduction in the number of lymphocytes in peripheral blood by seven days after separation from the mother. As discussed in the next section, this degree of alteration in the leukocyte pattern is associated with a significant reduction in the infant's ability to mount an antibody response to viral challenge.

While leukocyte redistribution has not been directly assessed in children during periods of separation and loss, it is highly likely that similar changes would be observed. It is almost axiomatic that these cellular changes will occur within minutes following any period of endocrine activation. In fact, studies of lymphocyte subsets in adult humans have indicated that cell trafficking is extremely responsive to brief periods of cognitive challenge or physical exercise lasting less than ten to twenty minutes (Landmann and others, 1984). Similarly, epinephrine injections in humans have been shown to cause marked changes in T helper and suppressor cell numbers over a two-hour period (Crary and others, 1983). Technical problems in marking T suppressor cells have prevented us from assessing lymphocyte subsets in infant squirrel monkeys, but in similar stress studies on aged rhesus monkeys we have demonstrated that there are marked decreases in both helper and suppressor cells during a seven-day period of mild disturbance (Ershler and others, 1988b).

Antibody Responses to Viral Challenge

Leukocyte redistribution by itself is a quantitative measure and does provide a functional indication of immune status. We, and others (Maier and Laudenslager, 1988), have found that the in vivo antibody response to antigenic challenge provides one of the most straightforward means to assess immune competence. In our first study, we chose to utilize the bacteriophage X174 because it is a benign virus with no clinical symptoms (Coe, Rosenberg, and Levine, 1988a). The antibody responses of infant squirrel monkeys separated from their mothers for one week were compared to those of undisturbed infants that were injected with the phage while they remained with their mothers. Antibody responses were determined at weekly intervals after injection of the virus. As can be seen in Figure 2, the separated monkeys showed a significantly reduced antibody response to the bacteriophage, especially at the fourteen-day point, which is the peak of the primary antibody response. The separated infants also tended to show smaller antibody responses when rechallenged with the virus two months later, but the robust nature of the secondary antibody response in all subjects resulted in a nonsignificant difference between the two conditions.

To establish the general validity of this finding, we conducted a similar study comparing antibody responses in another primate species,

Figure 2. Primary and Secondary Antibody Responses of Control Versus Maternally Separated Squirrel Monkey Infants

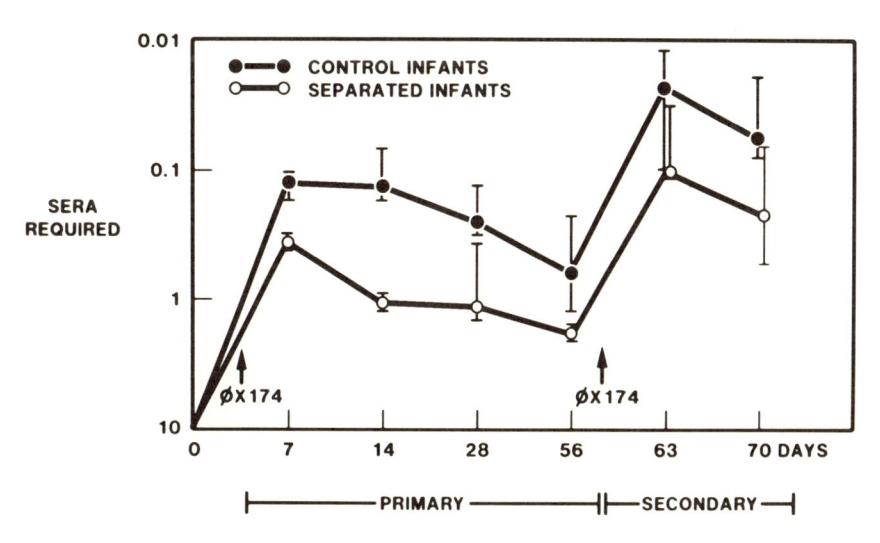

Note: Higher antibody levels are indicated by smaller serum volumes (μl) required to neutralize bacteriophage incubated with sera in the assay. Control $N = 6$; maternally separated $N = 4$.
Source: Coe, Rosenberg, and Levine, 1988a.

the rhesus monkey. This comparison was important because the squirrel monkey is a particularly stress-responsive species (Coe, Wiener, and Levine, 1983). Since their prolonged adrenal responses to separation lasting seven to fourteen days may tend to exaggerate immunological changes, it was necessary to demonstrate comparable findings in a primate species with an adrenal physiology more like that of humans. Antibody responses to the bacteriophage were measured in four undisturbed rhesus monkey infants that remained with their mothers, and in four infants injected at the end of a seven-day period of separation from their mothers. Although the magnitude of the difference in antibody responses was not as great in the rhesus monkey as it was in the squirrel monkey, separated infants did show a significantly lower primary antibody response than control infants.

These findings are in keeping with other studies on primates and rodents indicating that stressful events can hamper the ability of the individual to mount an antibody response. In fact, one of the earliest psychoimmunology studies using nonhuman primates demonstrated that juvenile vervet monkeys showed a smaller than normal antibody response to sheep red blood cells if injected during periods of noise and novelty stress (Hill, Greer, and Felsenfeld, 1967). More recently, it was reported that monkeys subjected to separations early in life mounted a smaller primary antibody response to keyhole limpet hemocyanin than monkeys that had not been disturbed in infancy (Laudenslager, Reite, and Held, 1986). Similar findings have been reported on mice that were exposed to early separation or premature weaning from the mother (Ackerman and others, 1988; Michaut and others, 1981; Raymond, Reyes, Tokuda, and Jones, 1986).

Antibody Responses in Different Separation Environments

While our previous studies established that the stress of maternal separation could alter antibody responses, they did not address the more theoretically interesting question of the specificity of the relationship between psychological state and immune response. Would psychological variables deemed important in modulating the separation response have a direct effect on our physiological measures of disturbance? To assess this type of question, we conducted a study on thirty-six squirrel monkey infants, entailing exposure to the bacteriophage under different housing conditions (Coe, Rosenberg, Fischer, and Levine, 1987). In addition to control subjects that remained with their mothers while they mounted the primary antibody response, blood samples were obtained at weekly intervals from infants exposed to the virus in five different separation conditions.

We replicated the previous observation that there is approximately a tenfold reduction of antibody titers in infants that had been housed alone for seven days. In addition, we showed that reunion of separated infants with their mothers on the day of injection does not restore the normal antibody response. That is, if the infant was in a disturbed state on the day of exposure to the virus, termination of the psychological disturbance did not result in a restoration of normal antibody synthesis. In contrast, modifying psychological aspects of the separation environment prior to virus exposure did significantly improve the antibody response. If the infant was either left in the home environment during the separation, by removing the mother instead of the infant, or provided with a familiar companion during the separation, it mounted a normal antibody response that was indistinguishable from control subjects. Thus, the immunological data supported our conclusion based on behavioral responses, that the separation environment strongly contributes to the infant's reaction to maternal loss.

These data on infant monkeys also concur with similar conclusions from studies on children. Separation reactions in children are usually less severe in the home environment and in the presence of supportive caregivers, whereas they tend to be aggravated in unfamiliar environments and in the presence of strangers (Robertson and Robertson, 1971; Weinraub and Lewis, 1977). Our results are also in keeping with one study of urinary cortisol levels in children, which did not find signs of adrenal activation following a brief separation in the home environment (Tennes, Downey, and Vernadakis, 1977). Separation of the monkey infant does evoke some adrenal activation even in the home environment, but of a smaller magnitude and considerably shorter duration than the response in unfamiliar environments (Coe, Wiener, and Levine, 1983). Presumably, adrenal activation would be greater in children separated from their mothers in a novel or threatening situation, such as a preoperative hospital setting or a first-time exposure to day-care (Gunnar, 1986).

Lymphocyte Proliferation

In ongoing studies, we have been assessing the effects of social separation on other immune responses. Although the in vitro lymphocyte proliferation test has not been our primary measure of interest, we did want to verify earlier reports on the effects of social separation in infant and juvenile macaque monkeys (Laudenslager, Reite, and Harbeck, 1982; Reite, Harbeck, and Hoffman, 1981). Since the previous research was conducted initially with juvenile monkeys subjected to peer separation, we also utilized removal of juvenile squirrel monkeys from a social group as our stimulus condition. Blood samples (3 ml) were obtained from six monkeys under three experimental conditions: (1) *Base:* previously undisturbed and living in a social group, (2) *3-hr.:* three hours after removal from the social group and housed alone in an unfamiliar cage, and (3) *24-hr.:* twenty-four hours after removal from the social group and housed alone (see Figure 3). Three weeks were allowed to elapse between experimental conditions to minimize the effect of prior blood sampling, although it should be acknowledged that the separation conditions did follow the baseline condition in this repeated-measures design.

Lymphocytes were separated from whole blood by density centrifugation. According to lymphocyte proliferation methods that we have standardized for monkeys (Ershler and others, 1988a, 1988b), the cells were then incubated for seventy-two hours with three concentrations of three different plant mitogens: concanavalin A (Con A), phytohemagglutinin (PHA), and pokeweed (PWM). In keeping with the prediction, marked decreases in lymphocyte proliferation were observed when the samples were obtained from separated juvenile monkeys. The decreases were statistically significant for both optimal and suboptimal concentrations of Con A and PWM, but not for PHA with this sample size. As can be seen in Figure 3, there was also a tendency for a slightly smaller reduction at twenty-four hours than at three hours postseparation. This suggestion of a transient change was supported in a follow-up study on lymphocyte proliferation in infants, assessed seven days after separation

Figure 3. Lymphocyte Proliferation Responses of Undisturbed Versus Socially Separated Juvenile Squirrel Monkeys

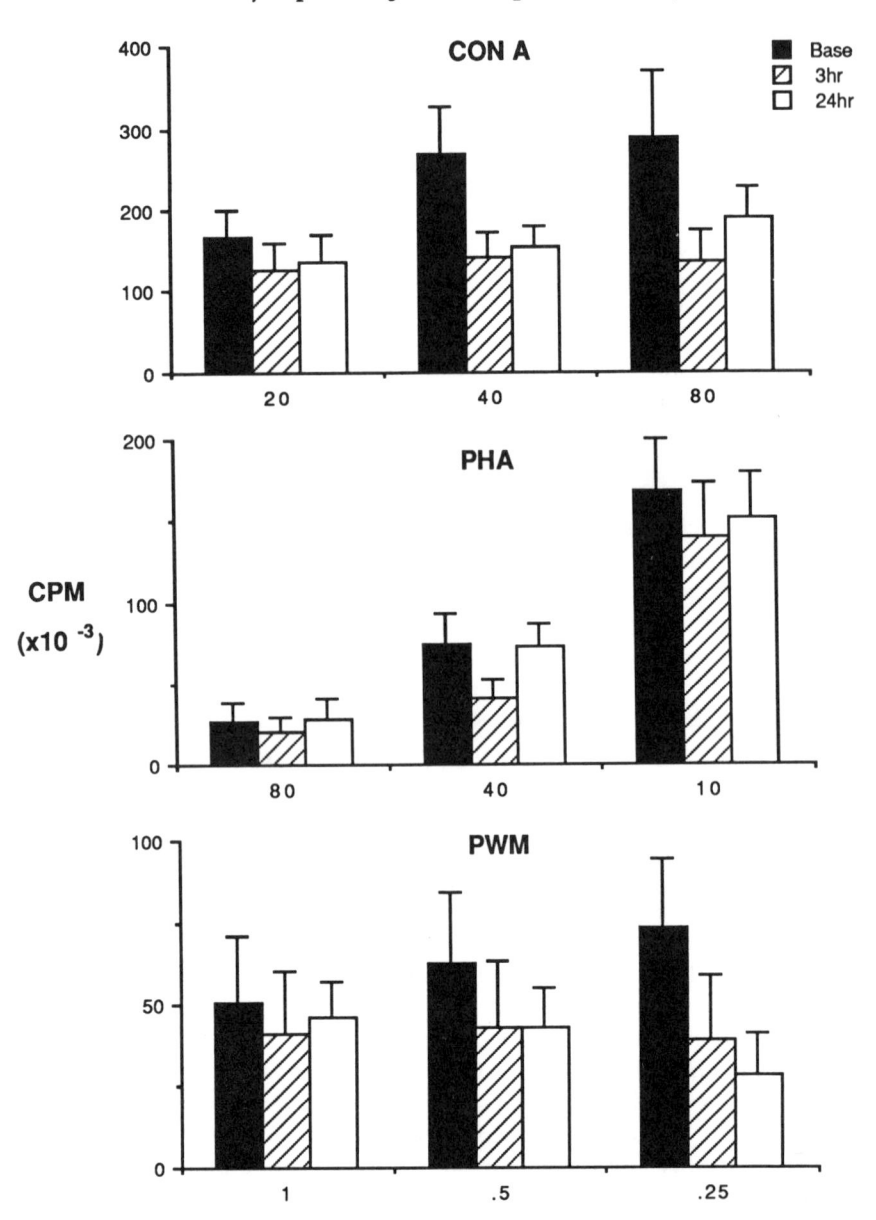

Note: Blood samples obtained prior to and three hours and twenty-four hours following separation from social groups, a repeated-measures design with $N = 6$. Decreased responses in separated infants can be seen at both suboptimal and optimal concentrations of three different mitogens: concanavalin A (CON A), phytohemagglutinin (PHA), and pokeweed (PWM).

from their mothers. In this experiment, we did not observe a significant decline in mitogen responses at the end of the week-long separation. Thus, while we replicated the finding that social separation can acutely affect lymphocyte proliferation responses, we failed to support the published reports of sustained decreases lasting up to two weeks (Laudenslager, Reite, and Harbeck, 1982). Recently, Laudenslager, Capitanio, and Reite (1985) qualified their earlier conclusion and now report that only those separated infants that become depressed will show a prolonged decrease in lymphocyte proliferation.

Although we could not demonstrate a week-long change in lymphocyte proliferation in separated squirrel monkeys, it should be mentioned that two studies on adult humans have documented decreases in response to mitogens for one to two months after loss of a spouse (Bartrop and others, 1977; Schleifer and others, 1983). Decreases in proliferation responses have also been described following other stressful life events, ranging from final exams to divorce (Glaser and others, 1987). Given these findings, our data may have suffered from one common problem with this particular immune test: day-to-day assay variation and subject variability in mitogen responses (see Maier and Laudenslager, 1988).

It is probable, however, that the greatest change in lymphocyte proliferation in infant monkeys occurs within the first few days after separation and that they return toward baseline levels within one to two weeks. In our research on other immune measures, we have found that a number of immune parameters follow this type of time course during periods of psychological disturbance. For example, in collaboration with N. Hall (University of South Florida), we have monitored levels of a hormone produced by the thymus gland, alpha-thymosin. This hormone has a number of important immune functions, including stimulation of the development of immature lymphocytes within the thymus. In one study we assessed alpha-thymosin in eighteen juvenile squirrel monkeys during periods of social separation lasting either four hours, two days, or seven days. Six monkeys were assigned to each condition, and the order of base and stress values was counterbalanced across subjects. While blood levels of alpha-thymosin were significantly decreased below normal at all three time points, the time course of the response appeared to be quite similar to our data on changes in lymphocyte proliferation. The greatest decrease was observed at four hours after removal of the juveniles from the social group, and alpha-thymosin levels were returning toward baseline values by the end of a week.

Hemolytic Complement Activity

For those readers who were hoping for a simple story describing a unidimensional relationship between social separation and immune suppression, the prior material may be somewhat disheartening. This section increases the complexity of the story a bit more by demonstrating that not all immune responses change in the negative direction. The next immune measure involves an aspect of humoral immunity known as hemolytic complement activity. Although we have not mentioned complement proteins previously, they are particularly important in the body's defense against bacterial infections. The complement proteins are produced by the liver and by macrophages and can act in a preprogrammed biochemical sequence to lyse bacteria or to activate different white blood cells. They are also involved in inflammatory processes and in facilitating the bonding of antibody and antigen. One common way of measuring the functional integrity of the complement system is to test the capacity of complement present in serum to lyse sheep red blood cells.

We have conducted two studies on the effects of social separation on hemolytic complement activity in the young squirrel monkey (Coe, Rosenberg, and Levine, 1988a). The first study assessed hemolytic complement activity in twenty-four infants on days one, seven, and fourteen after separation from their mothers. Small blood samples (< 1 ml) were obtained and spun in a refrigerated centrifuge; the sera were then stored in an ultracold freezer until assayed. Maternal separation did markedly affect hemolytic complement activity, but the change was in an upward direction. As compared to baseline conditions, there was a 25 to 33 percent increase in hemolytic complement activity. The increase was already apparent by day one and was sustained for the entire period of separation. Similar results were found in a second study on social separation in juvenile monkeys. Baseline and stress samples were obtained from eighteen squirrel monkeys, with six subjects assigned to each time point: four hours, two days, and seven days after removal from their social group (see Figure 4). At all time points, there was a significant increase in hemolytic complement activity.

At this juncture, we have not determined the physiological reason for these increases in complement activation, and the possible biological significance goes beyond the scope of this review. However, by way of partial explanation, let us mention that we believe that the changes in complement activity may be partially driving the other immune changes and that the increase may not be indicative of a positive health change. Hemolytic complement activity will also rise in response to tissue damage and will increase in the early stages of infection. When it occurs in this context, hemolytic complement activity is described as an acute phase reactant. Why the stressed monkey would show an increase in acute phase reactants is not clear. However, in support of this interpretation, we have recently determined that there are increases in other acute phase reactants, including haptoglobin and alpha-anti-trypsin, during the first twenty-four hours after separation. Further studies will be required to estab-

Figure 4. Hemolytic Complement Activity in Undisturbed Versus Socially Separated Squirrel Monkey Infants

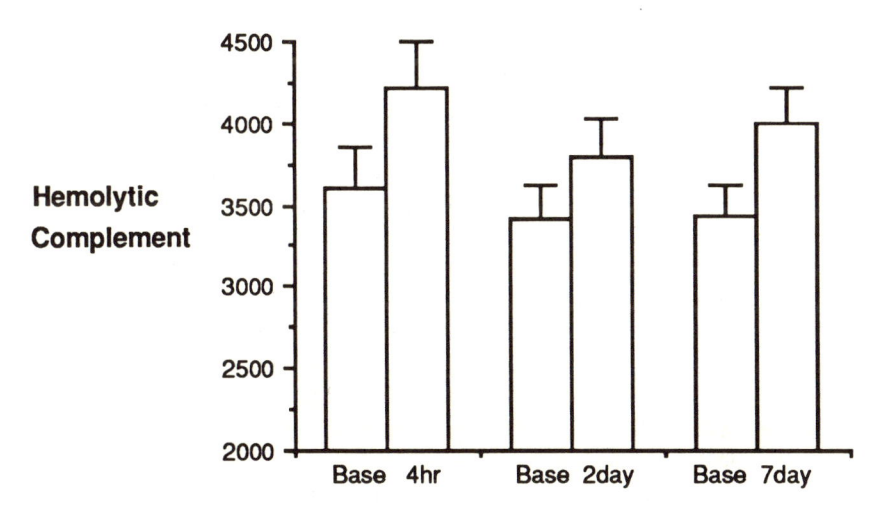

Note: Blood samples obtained prior to and either four hours, two days, or seven days following separation from social groups; $N = 6$ for each experimental condition.
Source: Coe, Rosenberg, and Levine, 1988a.

lish the linkage between these hematological parameters and the other immune measures we described earlier.

Delayed Hypersensitivity

Thus far, we have provided evidence that the emotional disturbance evoked by social separation can affect a number of immune responses. However, we have noted that there is temporal variation in these changes, and that some show increased rather than decreased activity. For two other measures, we have obtained similar data showing an upward direction of change. In this section, we consider the effects of maternal separation on another in vivo measure of immunity: delayed hypersensitivity. Normally, this measure is used by physicians to diagnose severe immune suppression, in which case there is a failure to show a skin reaction to the chemical challenge test. However, it can also be used in psychoimmunology studies, since stressful procedures during either the sensitization period or the recall test can influence the size of the cutaneous response. Therefore, we decided to evaluate whether separation of infant monkeys during either the sensitization or recall periods would alter redness and skin thickening at the site of the chemical application.

The infant monkeys were sensitized to an immunogenic chemical, dinitrochlorobenzene (DNCB), by five daily exposures. Each day 0.5 mg DNCB in a 25 µl drop of acetone was applied to their shoulder. Nine days later, each infant was reexposed to the DNCB to evaluate immunological memory and the ability to mount a response. Control subjects were sensitized and challenged while they remained with their mothers; others were sensitized while with their mothers but challenged on the day of separation (see Figure 5). Some were both sensitized and challenged while separated from the mother; still others were sensitized while separated but then reunited with mothers on the day of challenge. In all of the disturbed conditions, the separated and previously separated infants mounted a larger response than control subjects.

While a larger than normal cutaneous response may seem counterintuitive, it is important to reiterate that an increased immune response is not always the preferred outcome. The delayed hypersensitivity test is extremely simple, but the underlying immunological processes are quite complex. A larger than normal skin reaction may reflect a failure to appropriately regulate the immune response. It may be that nonspecific inflammatory processes, mediated through histamine, are exaggerated in the stressed infant, or that there is a failure of T suppressor cells to correctly turn off the immune response to DNCB once it is initiated.

Figure 5. Delayed Hypersensitivity Skin Response to DNCB by Control Versus Maternally Separated Squirrel Monkey Infants

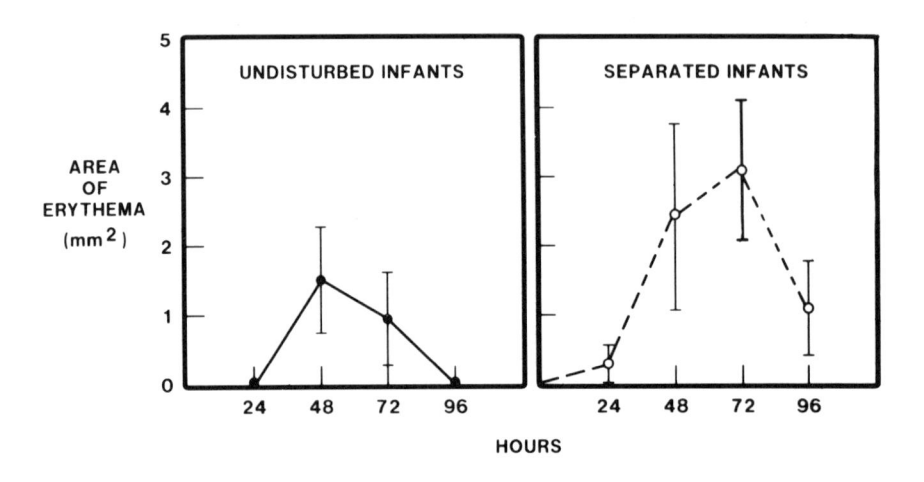

Note: DNCB is the immunogenic chemical dinitrochlorobenzene that elicits a skin reaction on reexposure. Control $N = 5$; maternally separated $N = 4$, separated on day of exposure.

Source: Coe, Rosenberg, and Levine, 1988b.

Examples of this type of aggravated reaction can be found in most dermatology textbooks, in the sections on stress-induced dermatitis and eczema or on stress-aggravated allergic reactions. At this time, we can only add the observation of increased delayed hypersensitivity responses to our growing list of altered immune measures in the separated infant.

Macrophage Responses

In this final section of the effects of acute separation, we consider another complex issue—the nature of immune responses during the recovery period. During prolonged periods of stress or following termination of a stressor, there may be a rebound in the immune responses deviating away from the original baseline (Monjan and Collector, 1977). Some theorists have even suggested that the role of adrenal cortisol is to return the individual back to normal immune function after it has been activated by other physiological systems, and that the inhibitory effects of corticosteroids on immune responses actually reflect an overshoot reaction (Munck, Guyre, and Holbrook, 1984). As in the previous research, the next experiments were designed to assess the impact of maternal separation on a particular immune parameter, in this case, one aspect of macrophage function. We have completed two experiments examining the ability of the blood monocyte/macrophage to become activated before, during, and after maternal separation.

In the first study, we assessed a measure of macrophage activity described as chemiluminescence (see Figure 6). When the macrophage becomes activated following exposure to bacteria or certain types of particles, it begins to produce a class of compounds, including hydrogen peroxide and superoxides. On the adaptive side, these compounds may have microbiocidal activity, assisting in the destruction of bacteria (Babior, 1978); but at high levels they may also cause damage to surrounding tissue. High levels of superoxides have been shown to damage lung tissue in adult respiratory distress syndromes, and high levels of macrophage chemiluminescence occurs in diseases, such as ulcerative colitis (Kitahora and others, 1988). Thus, it seemed to be a potentially important measure to evaluate following periods of psychological disturbance. In our study, the oxidative or respiratory burst of blood monocytes was assessed in vitro by stimulating the cells with zymosan for ninety minutes and then measuring the responses as light emission, using luminol and a scintillation counter.

Blood samples were obtained from seven mother-infant pairs under baseline conditions and twenty-four hours after separation of each dyad. Subsequently, the pairs were reunited, and additional samples were obtained at two weeks and two months after reunion. As in our other studies, social separation proved to be a potent source of psychological

Figure 6. Macrophage Chemiluminescence Responses of Squirrel Monkey Mother-Infant Pairs

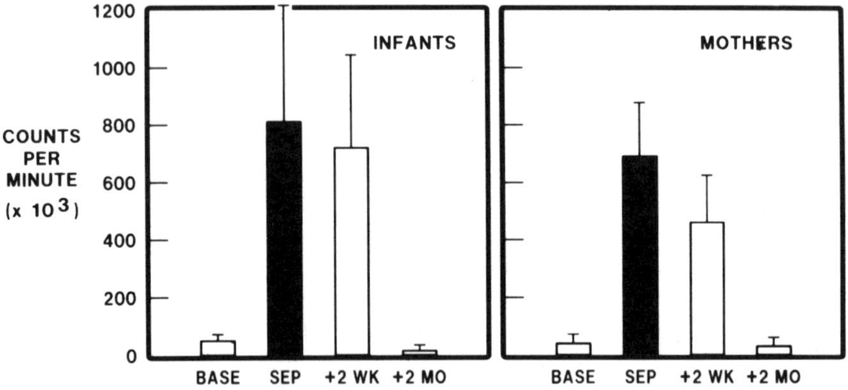

Note: Blood samples obtained prior to and after a twenty-four-hour separation and at two weeks and two months after reunion; mother-infant pairs $N = 7$.
Source: Coe, Rosenberg, and Levine, 1988c.

disturbance and physiological change. Marked increases in macrophage chemiluminescence were observed at the end of the twenty-four-hour separation and still persisted at two weeks after reunion of each dyad. Thus, the effect of separation on this immune measure lingered for two weeks after the signs of behavioral and endocrine disturbance had subsided. Moreover, the pattern of change was once again in the enhanced, rather than the negative, direction.

The finding of a two-week, postseparation effect was so intriguing that we designed a replication study. A new collaboration with R. Albrecht, C. Erickson, and P. Shult (University of Wisconsin) permitted us to directly assess the production of superoxides by blood monocytes with a cytochrome C reduction assay (Shult, Graziano, Wallow, and Busse, 1985). The design of the study was the same as before. Blood samples were collected from seven mother-infant pairs before, and for one month after, a twenty-four-hour period of separation. The cells were stimulated with either zymosan or phorbol-myristate-acetate, and superoxide release was measured at thirty-minute intervals for three hours. The data established unequivocally that monocyte superoxide production in the infant monkey was altered by the disturbance of maternal separation, and that the effect persists for several weeks after the end of the disturbance. However, the pattern of the data differed from the previous results. While we replicated the observation of a dramatic elevation over baseline levels for up to a month after reunion, superoxide release on the day of separation was decreased. At present, we do not have a good explanation for why the two assay approaches yielded different results on the day of separation, but the important finding is that some immune responses may be altered for several weeks after a twenty-four-hour stressor, an event of the type experienced by most individuals at some point in their life.

Immunological Effects of Abnormal Early Rearing

This observation of a relatively long-lasting effect of psychological disturbance on macrophage activity is especially important because a sustained change would be required to explain the possible link between stressful life events and subsequent disease. Retrospective studies of pediatric patient populations have suggested that stressful life events over a period of two years prior to disease onset can contribute to disease incidence and progression (Greene and Miller, 1958; Heisel, 1972: Jacobs and Charles, 1980; Laudenslager and Reite, 1984). Yet, in most physiological studies the observed changes are too small or too brief to mediate the disease vulnerability. Our best evidence for the existence of this type of sustained physiological alteration comes not from the study of acute separation responses but rather from examination of the long-term effects of different types of maternal rearing.

In the next study, we were initially interested in comparing monkey infants hand-raised by humans in a nursery facility to monkeys that were normally reared by their mothers. Based on our previous studies on the effects of acute separation from the mother, one would be inclined to predict a strong influence of such a marked deviation from the normal, nurturant environment. We knew from years of previous research on nursery-reared monkeys that the monkeys would show extensive behavioral abnormalities, in addition to some signs of endocrine dysfunction, because they had developed in the absence of normal social stimulation (Champoux and others, in press; Kraemer, Ebert, Schmidt, and McKinney, in press; Martin, Sackett, Gunderson, and Goodlin-Jones, 1988; Sackett and others, 1973). However, no aspect of immune functioning had been studied in the nursery-reared infant.

In the first phase of the study, we examined lymphocyte proliferation responses in sixteen juvenile rhesus monkeys, between thirteen and sixteen months of age: eight mother-reared monkeys that still remained with their mothers and eight nursery-reared monkeys (Coe, Lubach, Ershler, and Klopp, 1988). At this stage in our research program, we would not have been surprised by the occurrence of a small difference in responses, but we were struck by the magnitude of the elevated levels that we observed in the nursery-reared monkeys (see Figure 7). Not only were the mitogen responses increased, which was opposite to our predictions, but also the proliferation values were on the high end of the normal

**Figure 7. Lymphocyte Proliferation Responses
of Juvenile Rhesus Monkeys Reared Under Different Conditions**

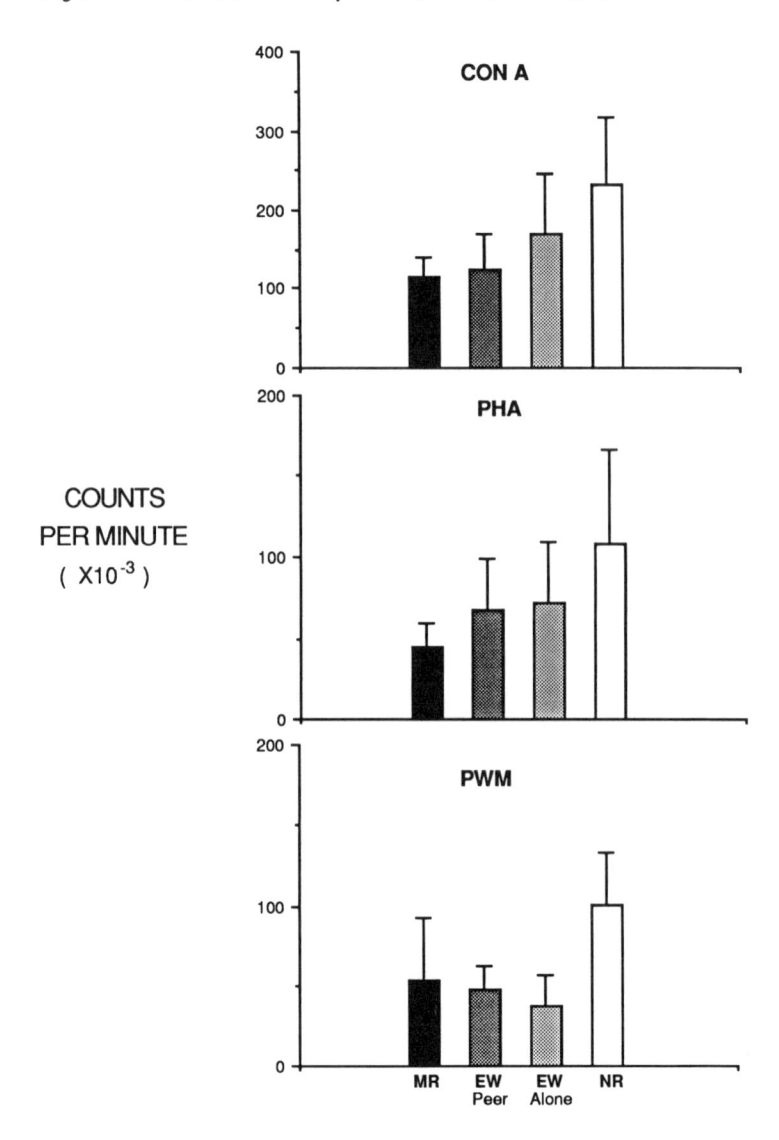

Note: Juvenile rhesus monkeys were reared under four different conditions: mother reared (MR), $N = 8$; nursery reared (NR), $N = 8$; weaned at six months of age and housed with peers (EW peer), $N = 6$; or weaned at six months of age and housed alone (EW alone), $N = 6$. Responses to three different mitogens: concanavalin A (CON A), phytohemagglutinin (PHA), and pokeweed (PWM).

Source: Coe, Lubach, Ershler, and Klopp, 1988.

range for the rhesus monkey. We have now followed these monkeys longitudinally through three and a half years of age. The responses to PHA and PWM showed an age-appropriate decrease into the normal range by two and a half years of age, while the high responses to Con A persisted for another year before they began to return to the normal range for the rhesus monkey. At present, we do not know if this pattern reflects the normal maturational sequence for the nursery-reared monkey, or if a social rehabilitation process mediated the return to normalcy. For humane reasons and to facilitate their normal socialization, the nursery-reared monkeys were housed in two small social groups after the first year's samples.

Although nursery rearing is an extreme condition and a human infant would not normally be raised in this manner, the findings may have some relevance to the increasing number of institutionalized babies in our society. Because of the AIDS epidemic and the increased use of cocaine by pregnant women, more babies are being reared in hospital settings. Moreover, we have also collected data on other rhesus monkeys from more benign rearing conditions, which support the conclusions about the importance of the early rearing environment. As can be seen in Figure 7, juvenile monkeys that had been experimentally weaned from their mothers at an early age, at six months instead of the more typical age of twelve months, also showed a similar tendency for elevated lymphocyte proliferation responses when tested as juveniles. Analyses of variance and post hoc tests showed that the twelve early weaned monkeys were statistically intermediate between the mother-reared and nursery-reared subjects. Although these findings might suggest that any alteration from normal maternal rearing results in a shift toward high mitogen responses, data from another important condition revealed that some rearing environments can result in inhibited responses. For the purposes of another study concerned with lactational amenorrhea, infant rhesus were repeatedly separated from their mothers for extended periods of time between three and seven months of age. Thereafter, they were left undisturbed with their mothers and weaned at one year of age. When we assessed blood samples obtained at twenty to twenty-three months of age, we found that lymphocyte proliferation responses to PHA were markedly below the normal range. That is, each of the assessed rearing conditions resulted in a different pattern of lymphocyte responses in the juvenile monkey. While the most extreme deviation from the normal pattern occurred in the behaviorally abnormal infants from the nursery environment, each rearing condition resulted in a distinctive profile.

General Considerations

This brief review of the effects of maternal separation and early rearing conditions on immune responses clearly shows that psychological disturbance can alter the immune system of the primate infant. The current findings extend an earlier finding on alterations in lymphocyte proliferation responses to a number of other immune parameters (Laudenslager, Reite, and Harbeck, 1982; Reite, Harbeck, and Hoffman, 1981). The data also concur with a much larger literature on the immunological effects of early separation and weaning in rodents and farm animals (LaBarba, 1970; Kelley, 1980; Solomon, Levine, and Kraft, 1968). Collectively, the studies attest to the potentially long-lasting effects of traumatic early life events on both in vivo and in vitro immune responses. Notwithstanding this substantial data base, there is a clear need for additional studies to characterize the nature of the changes in immune responses in greater detail. For many of the immune responses we have described, only one or two experiments were conducted, focusing on a particular time point. It should be apparent from our review that a more comprehensive analysis of the time course is required to understand the potential biological and clinical significance of a change in any given immune parameter.

In this regard, it should be reiterated that the health significance of transient changes in many of these immune responses has not been established. This point is especially important when the observed changes last only a few days and the altered responses still remain within the normal range of healthy individuals. For many of these assays, we do not know when a quantitative change translates into disease susceptibility. Our monkeys did not become clinically ill from either the separation or the resulting immunological changes. However, it should be emphasized that the laboratory environment is a relatively benign one, comparatively free of disease-causing pathogens. The data on decreased antibody responses in the separated infants suggests that they might show a heightened susceptibility if exposed to infectious agents and a worse disease outcome. To test this hypothesis, one would have to administer a disease-causing pathogen, which is not feasible or humane in primate studies. Where this has been done in studies on rodents, stressful events have been shown to worsen parasitic infestations, to hamper the containment of tumor growth, and to result in heightened mortality to lethal agents (Ader, 1981). Based on the current findings, it will also be important to determine if the increased hemolytic complement activity, or the prolonged changes in macrophage superoxide release, result in any adverse physiological effects.

An effect of early separation and premature weaning on disease processes could also appear at considerably later dates beyond the time points studied in our research. Retrospective studies on pediatric populations who have developed leukemia, juvenile rheumatoid arthritis, and other autoimmune diseases indicate that stressful life events over a one- to two-year time period may contribute to the precipitation and progression of disease (Heisel, 1972; Laudenslager and Reite, 1984). Our greatest concern would not be for the effects of acute separation but rather for the significant changes that may be wrought by abnormal, early rearing environments. Because of either the emotional effects of nursery rearing or the absence of breast milk, we found that the nursery-reared monkey showed an abnormal lymphocyte proliferation response in the juvenile stage. If this deviation proves to be associated with the other endocrine, autonomic, and CNS differences found in nursery-reared monkeys, then we will have to posit an important role for the mother in the development of many physiological systems (Champoux and others, in press; Kraemer, Ebert, Schmidt, and McKinney in press; Martin, Sackett, Gunderson, and Goodlin-Jones, 1988; Sackett and others, 1973). Equivalent data on rodents have already suggested that the mother is important in determining setpoints for the autonomic nervous system, cortisol, and growth hormone release (Hofer, 1983; Levine, Haltmeyer, Karas, and Denenberg, 1967; Schanberg and Field, 1987). Even if these alterations in baseline physiological activity prove not to have adverse effects in infancy, they may predispose the animals to diseases later in the life span. Epidemiological studies in humans have suggested that an abbreviated duration of breast-feeding in infancy is associated with an increased predisposition for diabetes and some forms of cancer (Davis, Savitz, and Graubard, 1988; Mayer, Hamman, and Gay, 1988). The data may also have some bearing on the choice of rearing strategies for institutionalized babies. While this was not an issue of major concern a few years ago, the occurrence of more cases of pediatric AIDS, as well as "cocaine" babies, has created a new public health concern. One can also speculate about the contribution of early rearing events and psychological factors to the incidence of even routine diseases of childhood (Boyce and others, 1977).

At the basic science level, it will be important to delineate the physiological mechanisms involved in the mediation of these immune changes. Most researchers have been biased toward attributing the immune changes to endocrine factors, especially to the pituitary-adrenal hormones. New studies have begun to show the influence of many other hormones on immune responses, and the literature on the relationship between the autonomic nervous system and immune system is growing daily (Berczi, 1986; Lloyd, 1984). We know, for example, that the thymus, spleen, and lymph nodes receive innervation from the sympathetic nervous system and that changes in adrenergic activity can affect many basic immune responses. There are also a whole host of factors involved in the mediation of immune responses that are not normally considered as likely end points in psychological studies. For example, we know that prostaglandin synthesis and the release of cytokines can be affected at least indirectly by stressful events (Munck, Guyre, and Holbrook, 1984; Pavlidis and Chirigos, 1980). One of the great challenges for the field of psychoneuroimmunology will be to decipher this complex communication network.

Given the importance of these physiological processes, it is extremely encouraging that we were able to show that psychological variables, which modulate the behavioral and emotional aspects of the separation response, had a predictable effect on the resulting immune responses. Familiarity with the separation environment and the availability of social companions entirely ameliorated the effect of maternal loss on immune responses in several of our studies. These data support the view that an understanding of how the organism appraises an aversive event and of its options for coping is central to predicting stress physiology. Thus, the final conclusion of an investigation into the cellular effects of stressful life events is a reiteration of the importance of cognitive and social approaches to stress management. For the young organism, a supportive and nurturing environment is important not only for successful behavioral maturation but apparently also for the development of normal immune function and for physical health.

References

Ackerman, S. H., Keller, S. E., Schleifer, S. J., Shindledecker, R. D., Camerino, M., Hofer, M. A., Weiner, H., and Stein, M. "Premature Maternal Separation and Lymphocyte Function." *Brain, Behavior, and Immunity,* 1988, *2,* 161–165.

Ader, R. (ed.). *Psychoneuroimmunology.* New York: Academic Press, 1981.

Babior, B. M. "Oxygen-Dependent Microbial Killing by Phagocytes." *New England Journal of Medicine,* 1978, *298,* 658–661.

Bartrop, R. W., Luckhurst, E., Lazarus, L., Kiloh, L. G., and Penney, R. "Depressed Lymphocyte Function After Bereavement." *Lancet,* 1977, *1* (8015), 834–836.

Berczi, I. (ed.). *Pituitary Function and Immunity.* Boca Raton, Fla.: CRC, 1986.

Bowlby, J. *Attachment and Loss: Separation.* Vol. 2. London: Hogarth, 1973.

Boyce, W. T., Jensen, E. W., Cassel, J. C., Collier, A. M., Smith, A. H., and Ramey, C. T. "Influence of Life Events and Family Routines on Childhood Respiratory Tract Illness." *Pediatrics,* 1977, *60* (4), 609–615.

Cauchi, M. N. "Immune Responses in the Fetus and the Neonate." In M. N. Cauchi (ed.), *Obstetric and Perinatal Immunology.* London: Edward Arnold, 1981.

Champoux, M., Coe, C. L., Schanberg, S., Kuhn, C., and Suomi, S. J. "Hormonal Effects of Early Rearing Conditions in the Infant Rhesus Monkey." *American Journal of Primatology,* in press.

Coe, C. L., Lubach, G. R., Ershler, W. B., and Klopp, R. G. "Influence of Early Rearing on Lymphocyte Proliferation Responses in Juvenile Rhesus Monkeys." *Brain, Behavior, and Immunity,* 1988, *2,* 1–10.

Coe, C. L., Rosenberg, L. T., Fischer, M., and Levine, S. "Psychological Factors Capable of Preventing the Inhibition of Antibody Responses in Separated Infant Monkeys." *Child Development,* 1987, *58* (6), 1420–1430.

Coe, C. L., Rosenberg, L. T., and Levine, S. "Effect of Maternal Separation on the Complement System and Antibody Responses in Infant Primates." *International Journal of Neuroscience,* 1988a, *40,* 289–302.

Coe, C. L., Rosenberg, L. T., and Levine, S. "Immunological Consequences of Psychological Disturbance and Maternal Loss in Infancy." In C. Rovee-Collier and L. P. Lipsitt (eds.), *Advances in Infancy Research.* Vol. 5. Norwood, N.J.: Ablex, 1988b.

Coe, C. L., Rosenberg, L. T., and Levine, S. "Prolonged Effect of Psychological Disturbance on Macrophage Chemiluminescence in the Squirrel Monkey." *Brain, Behavior, and Immunity,* 1988c, *2,* 151-160.

Coe, C. L., and Scheffler, J. "Utility of Immune Measures for Evaluating Psychological Well-Being in Nonhuman Primates." *Zoo Biology,* 1989, *suppl. 1,* 89-100.

Coe, C. L., Wiener, S. G., and Levine, S. "Psychoendocrine Responses of Mother and Infant Monkeys to Disturbance and Separation." In L. A. Rosenblum and H. Moltz (eds.), *Symbiosis in Parent-Offspring Interactions.* New York: Plenum, 1983.

Cohen, J. J., and Crnic, L. "Behavior, Stress and Lymphocyte Redistribution." In E. L. Cooper (ed.), *Stress, Immunity, and Aging.* New York: Marcel Dekker, 1984.

Crary, B., Borysenko, M., Sutherland, D. C., Kutz, I., Borysenko, J. Z., and Benson, H. "Decrease in Mitogen Responsiveness of Mononuclear Cells from Peripheral Blood After Epinephrine Administration in Humans." *Journal of Immunology,* 1983, *130,* 694-697.

Davis, M. K., Savitz, D. A., and Graubard, B. I. "Infant Feeding and Childhood Cancer." *Lancet,* 1988, *2* (8607), 365-368.

Ershler, W. B., Coe, C. L., Gravenstein, S., Schultz, K. T., Klopp, R. G., Meyer, M., and Houser, W. D. "Aging and Immunity in Nonhuman Primates. Part 1: Effects of Age and Gender on Cellular Immune Function in Rhesus Monkeys (*Macaca mulatta*)." *American Journal of Primatology,* 1988a, *15,* 181-188.

Ershler, W. B., Coe, C. L., Laughlin, N., Klopp, R. G., Gravenstein, S., Roecker, E. B., and Schultz, K. T. "Aging and Immunity in Nonhuman Primates. Part 2: Lymphocyte Response in Thymosin-Treated Middle-Aged Monkeys." *Journal of Gerontology,* 1988b, *43* (5), B142-146.

Glaser, R., Rice, J., Sheridan, J., Fertel, R., Stout, J., Speicher, C., Pinsky, D., Kotur, M., Post, A., Beck, M., and Kiecolt-Glaser, J. "Stress-Related Immune Suppression: Health Implications." *Brain, Behavior, and Immunity,* 1987, *1* (1), 7-21.

Greene, W. A., and Miller, G. "Psychological Factors and Reticulo-Endothelial Disease. Part 4: Observations on a Group of Children and Adolescents with Leukemias. An Interpretation of Disease Development in Terms of Mother-Child Unit." *Psychosomatic Medicine,* 1958, *10,* 124-144.

Gunnar, M. R. "Human Developmental Psychoendocrinology: A Review of Research on Neuroendocrine Responses to Challenge and Threat in Infancy and Childhood." In M. Lamb, A. Brown, and B. Rogoff (eds.), *Advances in Developmental Psychology.* Vol. 4. Hillsdale, N.J.: Erlbaum, 1986.

Harlow, H. F., and Zimmermann, R. R. "Affectional Responses in the Infant Monkey." *Science,* 1959, *130,* 421-432.

Heisel, J. S. "Life Changes as Etiologic Factors in Juvenile Rheumatoid Arthritis." *Journal of Psychiatric Research,* 1972, *16,* 411-420.

Hill, C. W., Greer, W. E., and Felsenfeld, O. "Psychological Stress, Early Responses to Foreign Protein, and Blood Cortisol in Vervets." *Psychosomatic Medicine,* 1967, *24,* 279-283.

Hofer, M. A. "The Mother-Infant Interaction as a Regulator of Infant Physiology and Behavior." In L. A. Rosenblum and H. Moltz (eds.), *Symbiosis in Parent-Offspring Interactions.* New York: Plenum, 1983.

Jacobs, T. J., and Charles, E. "Life Events and the Occurrence of Cancer in Children." *Psychosomatic Medicine,* 1980, *42,* 11-24.

Kelley, K. W. "Stress and Immune Function: A Bibliographic Review." *Annales Recharche Veterinaire*, 1980, *11* (4), 445-478.

Kitahora, T., Suzuki, K., Asakura, H., Yoshida, T., Suematsu, M., Watanabe, M., Aiso, S., and Tsuchiya, M. "Active Oxygen Species Generated by Monocytes and Polymorphonuclear Cells in Crohn's Disease." *Digestive Disease Science*, 1988, *33* (8), 951-955.

Kraemer, G. W., Ebert, M. H., Schmidt, D., and McKinney, W. T. "Effect of Different Social Rearing Conditions on Cerebrospinal Fluid, Norepinephrine, and Biogenic Amine Metabolites in Rhesus Monkeys." *Neuropsychopharmacology*, in press.

LaBarba, R. C. "Experiential and Environmental Factors in Cancer: A Review of Research with Animals." *Psychosomatic Medicine*, 1970, *32*, 259-276.

Landmann, R. M., Muller, F. B., Perini, C., Wesp, M., Erne, P., and Buhler, F. R. "Changes in Immunoregulatory Cells Induced by Psychological and Physical Stress: Relation to Catecholamines." *Clinical Experimental Immunology*, 1984, *58*, 127-135.

Laudenslager, M. L., Capitanio, J. P., and Reite, M. "Possible Effects of Early Separation Experiences on Subsequent Immune Function in Adult Macaque Monkeys." *American Journal of Psychiatry*, 1985, *142*, 862-864.

Laudenslager, M. L., and Reite, M. R. "Loss and Separations: Immunological Consequences and Health Implications." In P. Shaver (ed.), *Review of Personality and Social Psychology*. Newbury Park, Calif.: Sage, 1984.

Laudenslager, M. L., Reite, M. R., and Harbeck, R. J. "Suppressed Immune Response in Infant Monkeys Associated with Maternal Separation." *Behavioral Neural Biology*, 1982, *36*, 40-48.

Laudenslager, M. L., Reite, M. R., and Held, P. E. "Early Mother/Infant Separation Experiences Impair the Primary but Not the Secondary Antibody Response to a Novel Antigen in Young Pigtail Monkeys." *Psychosomatic Medicine*, 1986, *48*, 304.

Levine, S., Haltmeyer, G. C., Karas, G., and Denenberg, V. "Physiological and Behavioral Effects of Infantile Stimulation." *Physiology and Behavior*, 1967, *2*, 55-59.

Lloyd, R. "Mechanisms of Psychoneuroimmunological Responses." In B. H. Fox and B. H. Newberry (eds.), *Impact of Psychoendocrine Systems in Cancer and Immunity*. Lewiston, N.Y.: Hogrefe, 1984.

Maier, S. F., and Laudenslager, M. L. "Inescapable Shock, Shock Controllability, and Mitogen Stimulated Lymphocyte Proliferation." *Brain, Behavior, and Immunity*, 1988, *2* (2), 87-91.

Martin, R. E., Sackett, G. P., Gunderson, V. M., and Goodlin-Jones, B. L. "Auditory Evoked Heart Rate Responses in Pigtailed Macaques (*Macaca nemestrina*) Raised in Isolation." *Developmental Psychobiology*, 1988, *21*, 251-260.

Mayer, E. J., Hamman, R. F., and Gay, E. C. "Reduced Risk of Insulin Dependent Diabetes Mellitus (IDDM) Among Breast-Fed Children: A Case-Control Study." *Diabetes*, 1988, *37* (12), 1625-1632.

Michaut, R. J., Dechambre, R. P., Doumerc, S., Lesourd, B., Deuillechabrolle, A., and Moulias, R. "Influence of Early Maternal Deprivation on Adult Humoral Immune Response in Mice." *Physiology and Behavior*, 1981, *26*, 189-191.

Mineka, S., and Suomi, S. J. "Social Separation in Monkeys." *Psychological Bulletin*, 1978, *85*, 1376-1400.

Monjan, A. A., and Collector, M. I. "Stress-Induced Modulation of the Immune Response." *Science*, 1977, *196*, 307-308.

Munck, A., Guyre, P. M., and Holbrook, N. J. "Physiological Functions of Glucocorticoids in Stress and Their Relation to Pharmacological Actions." *Endocrine Reviews*, 1984, *5*, 25-44.

Pavlidis, N., and Chirigos, M. "Stress-Induced Impairment of Macrophage Tumoricidal Function." *Psychosomatic Medicine*, 1980, *42*, 47-54.

Raymond, L. N., Reyes, E., Tokuda, S., and Jones, B. C. "Differential Immune Response in Two Handled Inbred Strains of Mice." *Physiology and Behavior*, 1986, *37*, 295-297.

Reite, M., and Field, T. (eds.). *Psychobiology of Attachment and Separation.* New York: Academic Press, 1985.

Reite, M., Harbeck, R., and Hoffman, A. "Altered Cellular Immune Response Following Peer Separation." *Life Sciences*, 1981, *29*, 1133-1136.

Robertson, J., and Robertson, J. "Young Children in Brief Separation: A Fresh Look." *Psychoanalytic Study of the Child*, 1971, *26*, 264-315.

Sackett, G. P., Bowman, R. E., Meyer, J. S., Tripp, R. L., and Grady, S. A. "Adrenocortical and Behavioral Reactions by Differentially Raised Rhesus Monkeys." *Physiological Psychology*, 1973, *1*, 209-212.

Schanberg, S. M., and Field, T. M. "Sensory Deprivation, Stress, and Supplemental Stimulation in the Rat Pup and Preterm Human Neonate." *Child Development*, 1987, *58*, 1431-1447.

Schleifer, S. J., Keller, S. E., Camerino, M., Thornton, J. C., and Stein, M. "Suppression of Lymphocyte Stimulation Following Bereavement." *Journal American Medical Association*, 1983, *250*, 374-377.

Selye, H. *Stress: The Physiology and Pathology of Exposure to Stress.* Montreal: Acta Medical, 1950.

Shult, P. A., Graziano, F. M., Wallow, I. H., and Busse, W. W. "Comparison of Superoxide Generation and Luminol-Dependent Chemiluminescence with Eosinophils and Neutrophils from Normal Individuals." *Journal Laboratory Clinical Medicine*, 1985, *106* (6), 638-645.

Solomon, G. F., Levine, S., and Kraft, J. K. "Early Experience and Immunity." *Nature*, 1968, *220* (5169), 821-822.

Tennes, K., Downey, K., and Vernadakis, A. "Urinary Cortisol Excretion Rates and Anxiety in Normal One-Year-Old Infants." *Psychosomatic Medicine*, 1977, *39*, 178-187.

Wiener, S. G., Bayart, F.E.S., Faull, K., and Levine, S. "Behavioral and Physiological Responses to Maternal Separation in the Squirrel Monkey." *Behavioral Neuroscience*, in press.

Weinraub, M., and Lewis, M. *The Determinants of Children's Responses to Separation.* Monographs of the Society for Research in Child Development, no. 42. Chicago: Society for Research in Child Development, 1977.

Christopher L. Coe is a professor in the Department of Psychology, University of Wisconsin.

Gabriele Lubach is a graduate student in the Department of Anthropology, University of Wisconsin.

William B. Ershler is an associate professor in the Departments of Hematology and Medicine, University of Wisconsin.

Name Index

Ackerman, S. H., 74, 88
Ader, R., 66, 68, 86, 88
Ainsworth, M.D.S., 11, 16
Aiso, S., 90
Albrecht, R., 82
Alistair, G. S., 23, 24, 30
Als, H., 9, 17, 26, 30, 40, 44
Anand, K.J.S., 34, 44
Anders, T., 5, 16, 35, 44
Anderson, G., 30
Asakura, H., 90
August, G. P., 5, 17

Baade, E., 5, 18
Babior, B. M., 81, 88
Ban, P., 52, 63
Barten, S., 33, 44
Bartrop, R. W., 77, 88
Bates, J. E., 33, 44
Bauer, C., 30, 31
Baumel, M. H., 52, 63
Bayart, F.E.S., 67, 91
Beck, M., 89
Bell, R. Q., 55, 62
Benson, H., 89
Berczi, I., 87, 88
Birns, B., 33, 44
Borysenko, J. Z., 89
Borysenko, M., 89
Bowlby, J., 65, 88
Bowman, R. E., 91
Boyce, W. T., 87, 88
Brazelton, T. B., 9, 16, 17, 20, 26, 30, 33, 45, 53, 62
Brennan, J., 30
Bridger, W. H., 33, 44
Bruner, J. S., 48, 62
Buhler, F. R., 90
Buss, A. H., 33, 45
Busse, W. W., 82, 91

Camerino, M., 88, 91
Campos, J. J., 33, 45, 49, 61, 64
Capitanio, J. P., 77, 90
Carter, D., 5, 17, 35, 46
Cassel, J. C., 88
Cauchi, M. N., 66, 88
Caudill, W., 43, 44, 45

Champoux, M., 67, 83, 87, 88
Charles, E., 83, 89
Chess, S., 33, 45, 46
Chirigos, M., 87, 91
Coe, C. L., 2, 10, 16, 47, 48, 63, 65, 67, 70, 71, 72, 73, 74, 75, 78, 79, 80, 82, 83, 84, 88, 89, 91
Cohen, J. J., 71, 89
Collector, M. I., 81, 90
Collier, A. M., 88
Condon, L., 17
Connors, J., 7, 9, 12, 16
Craig, K. D., 34, 35, 45
Crary, B., 72, 89
Crispen, H., 65
Crnic, L., 71, 89

D'Apolito, K., 34, 45
Davis, M. K., 87, 89
de Kloet, R., 4, 16
de Wied, D., 4, 16
Dechambre, R. P., 90
Dembroski, T. M., 47, 62
Denenberg, V., 87, 90
Derryberry, D., 33, 46, 50, 51, 64
Deuillechabrolle, A., 90
Diamond, A., 49, 62
DiPietro, J. A., 52, 53, 62
Dohrenwend, B. P., 47, 62
Donhowe, J., 7, 16
Dorian, B., 40, 45
Dougherty, L. M., 34, 45
Downey, K., 10, 12, 18, 75, 91
Dumerc, S., 90

Ebert, M. H., 67, 83, 87, 90
Eichler, L. S., 20, 30
Emde, R. N., 10, 16, 49, 61, 64
Eppinger, H., 52, 62
Erickson, C., 82
Erne, P., 90
Ershler, W. B., 65, 72, 75, 83, 84, 88, 89, 91
Evans, A. S., 41, 45

Faull, K., 67, 91
Felsenfeld, O., 73, 89
Fertel, R., 89

Field, T., 1, 19, 20, 21, 22, 24, 25, 26, 27, 28, 29, 30, 31, 34, 35, 45, 54, 62, 66, 67, 87, 91
Fisch, R., 7, 8, 9, 16, 17, 34, 42, 45, 47, 48, 63
Fischer, M., 74, 88
Folkman, S., 48, 63
Fox, N., 1, 47, 51, 52, 54, 55, 62, 64
Franck, L. S., 35, 45
Frankenhaueser, M., 3, 16
Freedman, D. G., 43, 45
Freedman, N., 43, 45
Frost, L., 43, 45
Fust, S., 9, 16, 25, 30

Gaiter, J. L., 21, 30
Garcia, R., 30
Garcia-Coll, C., 54, 62
Garfinkel, P. E., 40, 45
Gay, E. C., 87, 90
Gelles, M., 55, 62
Glaser, R., 69, 77, 89
Glasgow, A. M., 5, 17
Goldsmith, H. H., 33, 45, 49, 62
Goldsmith, W., 7, 17
Goldson, E., 27, 30, 34, 35, 45
Gonzales, C., 10, 16
Goodlin, B., 10, 16
Goodlin-Jones, B. L., 67, 83, 87, 90
Gorsuch, R. L., 20, 31
Gottesman, I. I., 49, 62
Gottfried, A. W., 21, 30
Gouin-Decarie, T., 49, 55, 64
Grady, S. A., 91
Graubard, B. I., 87, 89
Gravenstein, S., 89
Graziano, F. M., 82, 91
Greenberg, R., 30
Greene, W. A., 83, 89
Greenfield, N. S., 41, 45
Greer, W. E., 73, 89
Grossman, F. K., 20, 30
Grossman, K. A., 14, 17
Grossman, P., 54, 63
Grunau, R.V.E., 35, 45
Gunderson, V. M., 67, 83, 87, 90
Gunnar, M. R., 1, 3, 6, 7, 8, 9, 10, 11, 12, 13, 14, 15, 16, 17, 18, 25, 30, 34, 42, 45, 47, 48, 63, 75, 89
Guyre, P. M., 3, 17, 81, 87, 91

Hall, N., 77
Haltmeyer, G. C., 87, 90

Hamman, R. F., 87, 90
Harbeck, R., 68, 75, 77, 86, 90, 91
Harlow, H. F., 65, 66, 89
Harmon, R., 16
Harper, R. M., 54, 63
Heisel, J. S., 83, 86, 89
Held, P. E., 74, 90
Hellman, L., 16, 44
Hembree, E. A., 34, 45, 61, 63
Hennessy, J., 3, 13, 17
Herd, J. A., 47, 62
Hertsgaard, L., 11, 13, 14, 15, 16
Hess, L., 52, 62
Hickey, P. R., 34, 44
Hill, C. W., 73, 89
Hinde, R. A., 45
Hodgman, J., 63
Hofer, M. A., 87, 88, 89
Hoffman, A., 75, 86, 91
Holbrook, N. J., 3, 17, 81, 87, 91
Holmes, T. H., 41, 43, 45
Hoppenbrouwers, T., 63
Houser, W. D., 89
Huebner, R. R., 34, 45, 61, 63
Hughes, I. A., 4, 17
Hung, W., 5, 17

Ignatoff, E., 30
Isensee, J., 7, 8, 9, 12, 16, 25, 30
Izard, C. E., 34, 45, 61, 63

Jacobs, T. J., 83, 89
Jay, S., 28, 30
Jensen, E. W., 88
Jih, F., 53, 63
Jones, B. C., 74, 91

Kagan, J., 51, 54, 62, 63
Karas, G., 87, 90
Kasl, S. V., 41, 45
Katonah, P. G., 53, 63
Kaufman, I. C., 64
Keller, S. E., 88, 91
Kelley, K. W., 68, 86, 90
Kestenbaum, R., 17
Kiecolt-Glaser, J., 89
Kiloh, L. G., 88
Kitahora, T., 81, 90
Klopp, R. G., 83, 84, 88, 89
Koenig, K., 16
Kopp, C. B., 52, 63
Korner, A., 26, 30
Korsvik, S., 7, 16

Name Index

Kotur, M., 89
Kraemer, G. W., 67, 83, 87, 90
Kraft, J. K., 86, 91
Kream, J., 16, 44
Kringlen, E., 49, 64
Kuhn, C., 30, 31, 88
Kutz, I., 89

LaBarba, R. C., 68, 86, 90
Lacey, B. C., 52, 63
Lacey, J. I., 52, 63
Landmann, R. M., 72, 90
Larson, M., 11, 14, 15, 16
Larson, S. K., 52, 53, 62
Laub, K. W., 33, 43, 44
Laudenslager, M. L., 68, 72, 74, 75, 77, 83, 86, 90
Laughlin, N., 89
Lazarus, L., 88
Lazarus, R., 48, 63
Lehman, H., 13, 16
Lesourd, B., 90
Lester, B. M., 9, 17, 26, 30, 40, 42, 46
Levine, S., 3, 5, 10, 13, 16, 17, 18, 41, 46, 47, 48, 63, 65, 67, 72, 73, 74, 75, 78, 79, 80, 82, 86, 87, 88, 89, 90, 91
Lewis, M., 1, 2, 12, 14, 17, 33, 34, 38, 43, 46, 52, 63, 75, 91
Lind, J., 42, 46
Linnemeyer, S. A., 53, 63
Lipsitt, L. P., 33, 46
Lloyd, R., 87, 90
Long, J. G., 23, 24, 30
Lubach, G., 65, 83, 84, 88, 91
Lucey, J., 21, 23, 24, 30
Luckhurst, E., 88
Lushene, R. E., 20, 31

McCabe, P. M., 54, 64
McCall, R. B., 45
MacDougall, J. M., 47, 62
McGinty, D. J., 63
McKinney, W. T., 67, 83, 87, 90
McMahon, R. J., 34, 45
Maier, S. F., 72, 77, 90
Malone, S., 7, 16, 17, 34, 42, 45, 47, 48, 63
Mangelsdorf, S., 11, 14, 15, 16
Martin, R. E., 67, 83, 87, 90
Marvinney, D., 8, 9, 16
Mason, J., 4, 18
Masuda, M., 41, 43, 45
Matheny, A. P., 11, 17
Maughn, G., 7, 17

Mayer, E. J., 87, 90
Meindel, E., 14, 17
Mendoza, S., 10, 16
Metcalf, D., 16
Meyer, J. S., 91
Meyer, M., 89
Michaelsson, K., 42, 46
Michaut, R. J., 74, 90
Miller, G., 83, 89
Mineka, S., 67, 90
Mischel, W., 43, 46
Monjan, A. A., 81, 90
Morison, J. D., 34, 45
Morrow, C., 22, 24, 25, 31
Moulias, R., 90
Muller, F. B., 90
Munck, A., 3, 17, 81, 87, 91

Niederman, J. C., 41, 45
Nystrom, J., 30

Parkaneu, T. J., 46
Pauley, J. D., 64
Pavlidis, N., 87, 91
Pearlman, W., 7, 17
Penney, R., 88
Perini, C., 90
Philip, A.G.S., 23, 24, 30
Pinsky, D., 89
Plomin, R., 33, 45
Porges, S. W., 48, 52, 53, 54, 55, 62, 63, 64
Porter, F. L., 48, 64
Posner, M. I., 50, 52, 64
Post, A., 89
Potter, H. D., 7, 17
Prechtl, H. F., 42, 46
Provost, M. A., 49, 55, 64

Quetel, T. A., 30

Ramey, C. T., 88
Raymond, L. N., 74, 91
Read, G., 4, 17
Reite, M., 48, 64, 66, 67, 68, 74, 75, 77, 83, 86, 90, 91
Reyes, E., 74, 91
Reznick, J. S., 51, 54, 62, 63
Riad-Fahmy, D., 4, 17
Rice, J., 89
Richards, J. E., 53, 54, 64
Riese, M. L., 33, 46
Roberts, J., 31

Robertson, J., 74, 91
Roecker, E. B., 89
Roessler, R., 41, 45
Roffwarg, H., 16, 44
Rosario, M., 30
Rosberg, G., 46
Rose, R. M., 3, 5, 17
Rosenberg, L., 65, 72, 73, 74, 78, 79, 80, 82, 88, 89
Rosley, A. P., 41, 45
Rothbart, M. K., 33, 45, 46, 49, 50, 51, 52, 64

Sachar, E., 16, 44
Sackett, G. P., 67, 83, 87, 90, 91
Sandberg, D., 30
Savitz, D. A., 87, 89
Scafidi, F., 30, 31
Schanberg, S., 30, 31, 87, 88, 91
Scheffler, J., 70, 71, 89
Schilmoeller, G. L., 33, 43, 44
Schleifer, S. J., 77, 88, 91
Schmidt, D., 67, 83, 87, 90
Schultz, K. T., 89
Selye, H., 3, 4, 17, 70, 91
Sheridan, J., 89
Shields, J. L., 47, 62
Shindledecker, R. D., 88
Short, R., 64
Shult, P. A., 82, 91
Sirvio, P., 42, 46
Smith, A. H., 88
Smotherman, W., 10, 16
Snellman, L., 17
Snidman, N., 51, 63
Solomon, G. F., 86, 91
Spangler, G., 14, 17
Speicher, C., 89
Spielberger, C. D., 20, 31
Spizzirri, C. C., 34, 45
Stang, H., 7, 17
Stein, M., 88, 91
Stenberg, C. R., 49, 61, 64
Sterman, M. B., 63
Stifter, C. A., 52, 54, 55, 64
Stout, J., 89
Stringer, S., 30
Stubbe, P., 26, 31
Stynes, A. J., 64
Suematsu, M., 90
Suomi, S. J., 67, 88, 90
Sutherland, D. C., 89

Suzuki, K., 90
Sybulski, S., 7, 17

Talbert, L., 7, 17
Tennes, K., 4, 5, 10, 12, 17, 18, 35, 46, 75, 91
Tepperman, J., 3, 4, 18
Thomas, A., 33, 45, 46
Thomas, D., 12, 14, 17, 33, 34, 46
Thornton, J. C., 91
Tokuda, S., 74, 91
Torgensen, A. E., 49, 64
Tripp, R. L., 91
Tronick, E. Z., 26, 30
Tsuchiya, M., 90
Tucci, K., 31

Ursin, H., 5, 18

Vance, G., 7, 16, 34, 45, 47, 48, 63
Vega-Lahr, N., 30
Vernadakis, A., 10, 12, 18, 75, 91
Vuoreukoski, V., 46

Wagonfield, S., 16
Waldrop, M. F., 55, 62
Wall, L., 7, 9, 16
Wallow, I. H., 82, 91
Wasz-Hockert, O., 46
Watanabe, M., 90
Weiner, H., 88
Weinraub, M., 74–75, 91
Weinstein, H., 44, 45
Weller, G. M., 55, 62
Wenger, M. A., 52, 64
Wesp, M., 90
Widmayer, S., 30
Wiener, S. G., 67, 73, 75, 89, 91
Wienthes, K., 54, 63
Wilder, J., 14, 18
Wilson, C. D., 52, 63
Wilson, R. S., 11, 17
Winickoff, S. A., 20, 30
Wittag, B. A., 11, 16
Wolf, M., 26, 31
Worobey, J., 2, 33, 38, 43, 46

Yongue, B. G., 54, 64
Yoshida, T., 90

Zaskow, C., 34, 45
Zeskind, P. S., 42, 46
Zimmermann, R. R., 66, 89

Subject Index

Adrenocortical response, 1; and adult stress, 4-5; and cortisol, 3-4; individual differences in, 13-15; in newborns, 5-10; in normal infants, 15; in older infants, 10-12; and repetition, 12-13
Adrenocortical system. *See* Hypothalamic-pituitary-adrenocortical system
AIDS, 68, 85, 87
Anger response, 61
Antibody, 69
Antibody responses: in separation environments, 74-75; to viruses, 72-74
Apgar score, and reactivity, 40, 41
Autonomic patterning: measurement of, 53-54; and reactivity, 54-62

Birth order, and reactivity, 40
Birth weight, and reactivity, 40, 41

Children, and stress, 1
Circumcision, 7, 8, 48
Coping: individual differences in, 61; and pacifiers, 27-28
Cortisol, 3; and adult stress, 4-5; individual differences in, 13-15; in newborns, 5-10; in normal infants, 15; in older infants, 10-12; and repetition, 12-13; and stress, 47; and stress resistance, 3-4
Crying: and heelstick, 36; and newborn health, 40; and socialization, 43-44

Dampening, 33-34
Distress response, 61

Emotions. *See* Temperament
Eosinophil, 68

Frustration, 1; research on, 48-50; as stressor, 48

Gavage tube: feeding by, 27-28; insertion of, 22

Health, and reactivity, 40-43
Heelstick, 7; newborn reactivity to, 35-38; and oxygen tension, 23; and pacifiers, 27; paradigm of, 34-35; reactivity to, and health, 41-42
Hemolytic complement activity, 77-79
Hypersensitivity, 79-81
Hypothalamic-pituitary-adrenocortical system, 6

Immune system: and abnormal early rearing, 83-85; and early rearing, 85-88; function of, 68-69; and stress, 2
Immunity: and infant stress, 66; Selye's findings on, 3, 70
Infants: adrenocortical response in, 15; adrenocortical studies with, 10-12; immunity of, and stress, 66; and repetition, 12-13; research on frustration with, 48-50; and separation, 10-12, 14. *See also* Newborns; Premature neonates
Inoculations: adrenocortical response to, 12, 14-15; and distress or anger, 61; reactivity to, and health, 38, 41; and socialization, 43-44

Lester's State Regulation Scale, 9
Leukocyte, redistribution of, 70-72
Louisville Temperament Assessment, 11
Lymphocytes, 69; proliferation of, 75-77

Macrophage, 69; responses of, 81-83
Monkeys: separation response of, 10, 67-68, 70-85; and stress, 2
Mononucleosis, and personality, 41

Neonatal Behavioral Assessment Scale (NBAS), 9, 15, 53; and oxygen tension, 25; and touching, 29-30; and ultrasound, 20, 22
Neonatal intensive care unit (NICU), 19; alleviating stress in, 26-30; stresses in, 21-26
Nervous system, features of, 33-34
Neutrophil, 68
New experiences, adrenocortical response to, 13

Newborns: adrenocortical activity in, 5-10; reactivity of, 35-38, 40-43. *See also* Infants; Premature neonates

Oxygen tension, 22-23, 25

Pacifiers, and neonate stress, 27-28; withdrawal of, 55-57
Pregnancy anxiety, and ultrasound, 20-21
Premature neonate: alleviating stress of, 26-30; stresses for, 21-26
Prenatal characteristics, and reactivity, 39-40
Psychoneuroimmunology, 66

Reactivation, 33-34
Reactivity, 1; and autonomic patterning, 54-62; and health, 40-43; individual differences in, 43-44; of newborns, 35-38; and prenatal characteristics, 39-40; psychophysiology of, 52-53; stability of, 38-39; and temperament, 33-34, 50-52
Repetition, and adrenocortical response, 12-13
Research: on autonomic patterning and reactivity, 54-62; on children and stress, 1; on infant frustration, 48-50
Respiratory sinus arrhythmia, 53-54
Response: anger, 61; antibody, 72-75; distress, 61. *See also* Adrenocortical response

Saliva, and cortisol measurement, 4, 15. *See also* Adrenocortical response

Self-regulation, and temperament, 50-52
Separation, maternal, 48; adrenocortical response to, 10-12, 14; primate immunological response to, 67-68, 70-85
Socialization, and inoculation, 43-44
Spielberger State/Trait Anxiety Scale, and ultrasound, 20
Strange Situation Assessment, 11
Stress, 1; and adults, 4-5; alleviating, in NICU, 26-30; and children, 1; and cortisol, 3-4, 47; and frustration, 48; and immune system, 2; and individual differences, 13-15; and infant immunity, 66; measures of, 36; and newborns, 5-10; and NICU procedures, 21-26; and older infants, 10-12; for premature neonates, 21-26
Stress, fetal, 1; and NBAS, 25; and oxygen tension, 22-23; and ultrasound, 20-21
Swimming, adrenocortical response to, 13

Temperament, 33; and andrenocortical response, 14, 15; and nervous system, 33-34; and reactivity and self-regulation, 50-52; and vagal tone, 58
Threshold, 33-34
Touching, and neonate stress, 28-30
Tube feeding. *See* Gavage tube

Ultrasound, and fetal stress, 20-21

Vagal tone, and reactivity, 53-62
Virus, antibody responses to, 72-74

Ordering Information

NEW DIRECTIONS FOR CHILD DEVELOPMENT is a series of paperback books that presents the latest research findings on all aspects of children's psychological development, including their cognitive, social, moral, and emotional growth. Books in the series are published quarterly, in Fall, Winter, Spring, and Summer, and are available for purchase by subscription as well as by single copy.

SUBSCRIPTIONS FOR 1989-90 cost $48.00 for individuals (a savings of 20 percent over single-copy prices) and $64.00 for institutions, agencies, and libraries. Please do not send institutional checks for personal subscriptions. Standing orders are accepted.

SINGLE COPIES cost $14.95 when payment accompanies order. (California, New Jersey, New York, and Washington, D.C., residents please include appropriate sales tax.) Billed orders will be charged postage and handling.

DISCOUNTS FOR QUANTITY ORDERS are available. Please write to the address below for information.

ALL ORDERS must include either the name of an individual or an official purchase order number. Please submit your order as follows:
Subscriptions: specify series and year subscription is to begin
Single copies: include individual title code (such as CD1)

MAIL ALL ORDERS TO:
Jossey-Bass Inc., Publishers
350 Sansome Street
San Francisco, California 94104

Other Titles Available
in the New Directions for Child Development Series

CD44 Empathy and Related Emotional Responses, *Nancy Eisenberg*
CD43 Maternal Responsiveness: Characteristics and Consequences, *Marc H. Bornstein*
CD42 Black Children and Poverty: A Developmental Perspective, *Diana T. Slaughter*
CD41 Children's Mathematics, *Geoffrey B. Saxe, Maryl Gearhart*
CD40 Parental Behavior in Diverse Societies, *Robert A. LeVine, Patrice M. Miller, Mary Maxwell West*
CD39 Developmental Psychopathology and Its Treatment, *Ellen D. Nannis, Philip A. Cowan*
CD38 Children's Gender Schemata, *Lynn S. Liben, Margaret L. Signorella*
CD37 Adolescent Social Behavior and Health, *Charles E. Irwin, Jr.*
CD36 Symbolic Development in Atypical Children, *Dante Cicchetti, Marjorie Beeghly*
CD35 How Children and Adolescents View the World of Work, *John H. Lewko*
CD34 Maternal Depression and Infant Disturbance, *Edward Z. Tronick, Tiffany Field*
CD33 Children's Intellectual Rights, *David Moshman*
CD32 Early Experience and the Development of Competence, *William Fowler*
CD31 Temperament and Social Interaction in Infants and Children, *Jacqueline V. Lerner, Richard M. Lerner*
CD30 Identity in Adolescence: Processes and Contents, *Alan S. Waterman*
CD29 Peer Conflict and Psychological Growth, *Marvin W. Berkowitz*
CD28 Children and Computers, *Elisa L. Klein*
CD27 The Development of Reading Skills, *Thomas H. Carr*
CD26 Childhood Depression, *Dante Cicchetti, Karen Schneider-Rosen*
CD25 Analyzing Children's Play Dialogues, *Frank Kessel, Artin Göncü*
CD24 Children in Families Under Stress, *Anna-Beth Doyle, Dolores Gold, Debbie S. Moscowitz*
CD23 Children's Learning in the "Zone of Proximal Development," *Barbara Rogoff, James V. Wertsch*
CD22 Adolescent Development in the Family, *Harold D. Grotevant, Catherine R. Cooper*
CD21 Levels and Transitions in Children's Development, *Kurt W. Fischer*
CD20 Child Development and International Development: Research-Policy Interfaces, *Daniel A. Wagner*
CD19 Children and Divorce, *Lawrence A. Kurdek*
CD18 Children's Planning Strategies, *David Forbes, Mark T. Greenberg*
CD17 Developmental Approaches to Giftedness and Creativity, *David Henry Feldman*
CD16 Emotional Development, *Dante Cicchetti, Petra Hesse*
CD15 Children's Conceptions of Spatial Relationships, *Robert Cohen*
CD14 Children's Conceptions of Health, Illness, and Bodily Functions, *Roger Bibace, Mary E. Walsh*
CD13 Viewing Children Through Television, *Hope Kelly, Howard Gardner*
CD12 Cognitive Development, *Kurt W. Fischer*
CD11 Developmental Perspectives on Child Maltreatment, *Ross Rizley, Dante Cicchetti*

CD10	Children's Memory, *Marion Perlmutter*
CD9	Children's Play, *Kenneth H. Rubin*
CD8	Anthropological Perspectives on Child Development, *Charles M. Super, Sara Harkness*
CD7	Clinical-Developmental Psychology, *Robert L. Selman, Regina Yando*
CD6	Fact, Fiction, and Fantasy in Childhood, *Ellen Winner, Howard Gardner*
CD5	Intellectual Development Beyond Childhood, *Deanna Kuhn*
CD4	Social Interaction and Communication During Infancy, *Ina C. Uzgiris*
CD2	Moral Development, *William Damon*
CD1	Social Cognition, *William Damon*